Own It! 4

PROJECT BOOK

Simon Cupit

CAMBRIDGE
UNIVERSITY PRESS

CAMBRIDGE
UNIVERSITY PRESS

University Printing House, Cambridge CB2 8BS, United Kingdom

One Liberty Plaza, 20th Floor, New York, NY 10006, USA

477 Williamstown Road, Port Melbourne, VIC 3207, Australia

314–321, 3rd Floor, Plot 3, Splendor Forum, Jasola District Centre, New Delhi – 110025, India

79 Anson Road, #06–04/06, Singapore 079906

José Abascal, 56–10, 28003 Madrid, Spain

Cambridge University Press is part of the University of Cambridge.

It furthers the University's mission by disseminating knowledge in the pursuit of education, learning and research at the highest international levels of excellence.

www.cambridge.org
Information on this title: www.cambridge.org/9781108726672

First published 2020

20 19 18 17 16 15 14 13 12 11 10 9 8 7 6 5 4 3 2 1

Printed in Dubai by Oriental Press

A catalogue record for this publication is available from the British Library

ISBN 978-1-108-72667-2 Own it! Project Book Level 4
ISBN 978-84-1322-013-0 Collaborate Project Book Level 4

Additional resources for this publication at www.cambridge.org/ownit/resources

CONTENTS

AN INTRODUCTION TO PROJECT WORK

Welcome to your students' final year of study! How will project work help them prepare for life beyond secondary school?

Your students should now have the confidence to carry out different types of projects successfully. Most of them are familiar with all stages of the process and can complete the majority of the steps in English. The projects in Level 4 recycle students' previous knowledge in a motivating way, while allowing them to continue to develop their collaborative skills.

This book will guide you on how to make the most of project work and help students get ready for the next stages of their lives.

What is project work?

Imagine you and your class have just finished Unit 2 (*Changes*). Your students have learned vocabulary for parts of objects and practised using past tenses as well as *used to* and *would*. How can you review and expand on this topic? In this case, your students work in groups to create a museum exhibition.

Remember that project work involves students being responsible for their work and making decisions together. There is a realistic final outcome and a series of stages to follow that allow groups to explore how they can achieve their goals. The final aim is always a presentation stage. **> Presentation ideas p18**. Your role is to help this happen. As a result, students learn by doing and share memorable experiences.

Throughout the project work process, students develop a number of **life skills**. They learn to:

Create new ideas

Question actively

Use social skills

Think critically

Work collaboratively

Create

BENEFITS AND ADVANTAGES OF PROJECT WORK

✓ Personal advantages

- encourages **creativity** by promoting **different ways of thinking**
- increases **motivation** through challenge
- develops **autonomy** and a **sense of responsibility**
- increases natural **curiosity**
- improves **self-knowledge** through **self-evaluation**
- improves **communication skills** through teamwork
- involves family and friends in the **learning process**
- improves **interpersonal** relationships
- develops **life skills**

✓ Academic advantages

- allows teachers to deal with **mixed-ability** classes
- motivates whole-team cooperation and group work and promotes chances to **learn from one another**
- develops **planning** and **organisational skills**
- offers a '**flipped classroom**' approach
- **helps learning** through research and opportunities for deep thinking
- increases opportunities to **integrate cross-curricular** and **cultural topics**
- encourages **peer teaching** and **correction**
- enables students with **different learning styles** to help one another

✓ Language learning

- provides opportunities to **use language naturally**
- integrates all **four skills** (reading, writing, listening and speaking)
- allows for the use of **self- and peer-evaluation language**
- encourages research and **use of English out of the class**
- is learner-centred: students **learn language from one another**
- practises both **fluency** and **accuracy** through different types of presentations

Project work and the Cambridge Life Competencies Framework

How can we prepare our students to succeed in a changing world? We see the need to help students develop transferable skills, to work with people from around the globe, to think creatively, analyse sources critically and communicate their views effectively. However, how can we balance the development of these skills with the demands of the language curriculum?

Cambridge have developed the Cambridge Life Competencies Framework. This Framework reinforces project work, helping teachers recognise and assess the many transferable skills that project work develops, alongside language learning.

The Framework provides different levels of detail, from six broad Competencies to specific Can Do Statements. The Competencies are supported by three foundation layers.

Critical Thinking	Creative Thinking	Collaboration	Communication	Learning to Learn	Social Responsibilities

EMOTIONAL DEVELOPMENT AND WELLBEING	DIGITAL LITERACY	DISCIPLINE KNOWLEDGE

It then defines specific Core Areas. For example, here are the Core Areas for Collaboration :

Taking personal responsibility for own contribution to a group task.	Listening respectfully and responding constructively to others' contributions.	Managing the sharing of tasks in a project.	Working towards a resolution related to a task.

Then, there is a Can Do Statement for each Core Area. These will differ depending on the age of the students.

Competency
Collaboration

↓

Core Area
Managing the sharing of tasks in a project.

↓

Can Do Statements
- Follows the instructions for a task and alerts others when not following them.
- Explains reasons for suggestions and contributions.
- Takes responsibility for completing tasks as part of a larger project.

For more information, go to:
cambridge.org/elt

Level 4 Projects	Competency	Core Area	Can Do Statements
The culture project: a fact file Teacher's Resource Bank Unit 1	Social Responsibilities	Understanding and describing own and others' cultures	*Accepts others and shows respect for cultural difference; Makes informed comparisons between their own society and other societies.*
	Learning to Learn	Taking control of own learning	*Identifies helpful resources for their learning; Finds sources of information and help (online and in school).*
The history project: a retro museum exhibition Student's Book pp30–31	Learning to Learn	Practical skills for participating in learning	*Produces a revision plan to focus on key skills and knowledge in a systematic way; Uses metacognitive strategies (e.g. time management) to maximise learning.*
	Collaboration	Taking personal responsibility for own contributions to a group task	*Follows the instructions for a task and alerts others when there are problems; Takes responsibility for completing tasks as part of a larger project.*
The culture project: a poster Teacher's Resource Bank Unit 3	Creative Thinking	Creating new content from own ideas or other resources	*Responds imaginatively to contemporary events and ideas; Makes an assignment original by changing the task or adding new angles.*
	Critical Thinking	Synthesising ideas and information	*Selects key points from diverse sources to create a new account.*
The science project: an infographic Student's Book pp54–55	Critical Thinking	Evaluating ideas, arguments and options	*Distinguishes between fact and opinion; Identifies evidence and its reliability.*
	Collaboration	Managing the sharing of tasks in a project	*Works with others to plan and execute class projects; Ensures that work is fairly divided among members in group activities.*
The culture project: a travel blog Teacher's Resource Bank Unit 5	Creative Thinking	Participating in creative activities	*Encourages group members to make activities more original and imaginative; Participates in 'what if' thinking.*
	Communication	Using appropriate language and register for context	*Knows how to present points clearly and persuasively; Uses language for effect.*
The citizenship project: a leaflet Student's Book pp78–79	Social Responsibilities	Taking active roles including leadership	*In group work, makes consultative decisions; Encourages others to participate and contribute in projects.*
	Communication	Participating with appropriate confidence and clarity	*Starts and manages conversations with confidence; Uses facial expressions and eye contact appropriately.*
The culture project: a presentation Teacher's Resource Bank Unit 7	Communication	Managing conversations	*Can use simple techniques to start, maintain and close conversations of various lengths; Paraphrasing.*
	Social Responsibilities	Understanding personal responsibilities as part of a group and in society – including citizenship	*Is aware of positive behaviour in different groups; Makes informed choices (e.g. in relation to diet, exercise, etc.)*
The art and design project: an advert storyboard Student's Book pp102–103	Critical Thinking	Understanding and analysing links between ideas	*Distinguishes between main and supporting arguments; Identifies the basic structure of an argument.*
	Collaboration	Listening respectfully and responding constructively to others' contributions	*Listens to and acknowledges different points of view respectfully; Evaluates contributions from other students with appropriate sensitivity.*
The culture project: a traditional story Teacher's Resource Bank Unit 9	Learning to Learn	Practical skills for participating in learning	*Organises notes systematically; Uses notes to construct original output.*
	Creative Thinking	Creating new content from own ideas or other resources	*Writes or tells an original story given prompts or without prompts; Communicates personal response to creative work from literature.*

HOW TO USE THE *PROJECT* BOOK

See learning outcomes at a glance, as well as the skills students will develop and the resources and evaluation tools you may wish to use.

Manage student roles and responsibilities.

Monitor and check the skills that project work develops, mapped to the Cambridge Life Competencies Framework.

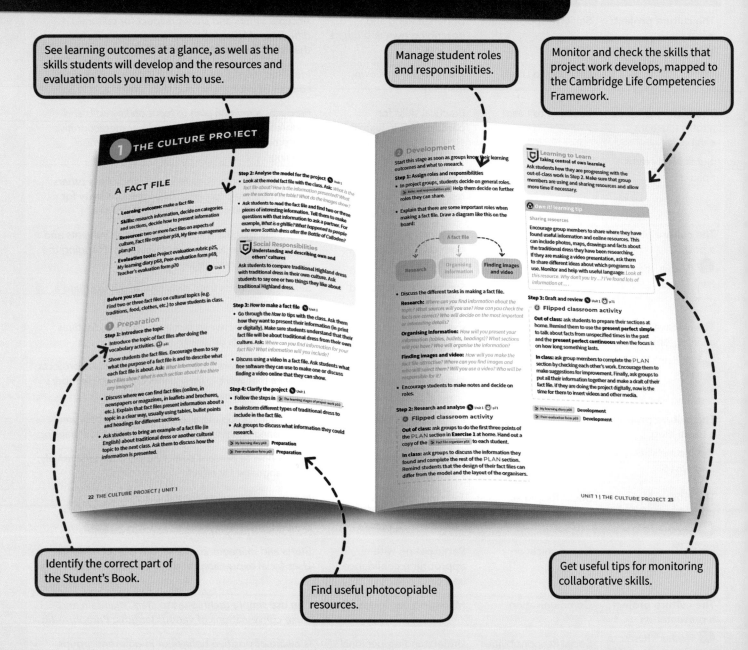

Identify the correct part of the Student's Book.

Find useful photocopiable resources.

Get useful tips for monitoring collaborative skills.

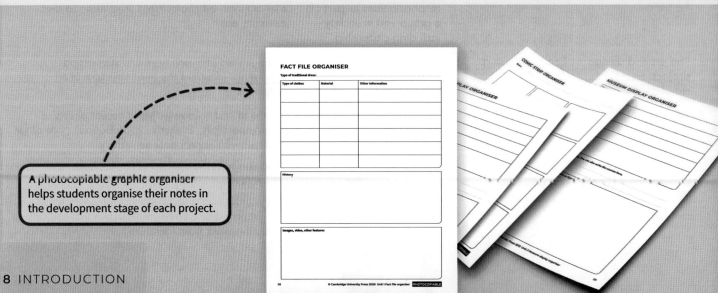

A photocopiable graphic organiser helps students organise their notes in the development stage of each project.

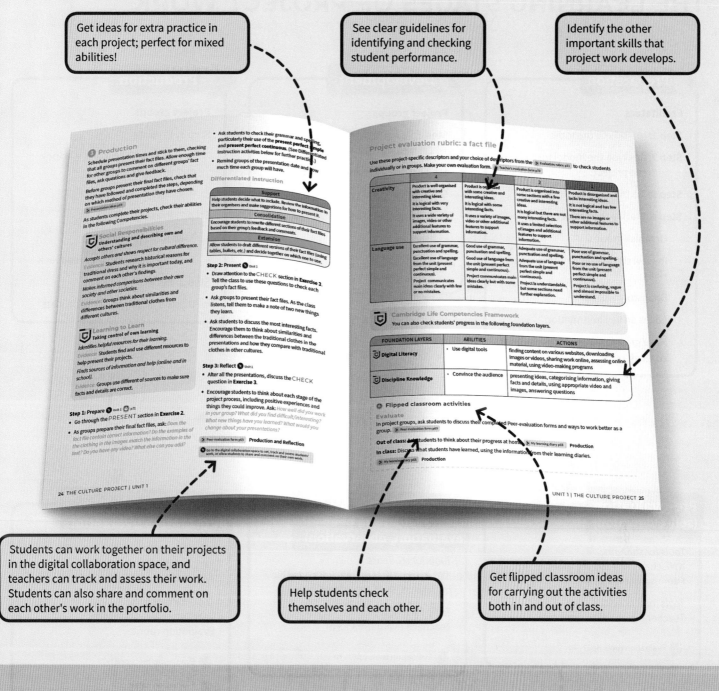

Get ideas for extra practice in each project; perfect for mixed abilities!

See clear guidelines for identifying and checking student performance.

Identify the other important skills that project work develops.

Students can work together on their projects in the digital collaboration space, and teachers can track and assess their work. Students can also share and comment on each other's work in the portfolio.

Help students check themselves and each other.

Get flipped classroom ideas for carrying out the activities both in and out of class.

Photocopiable assessment and time-management sheets help students work more independently.

THE LEARNING STAGES OF PROJECT WORK

1 Preparation

Facilitators

Step 1: Introduce the topic

Step 2: Analyse the model for the project

Step 3: Go through the *How to* tips

Step 4: Clarify the project

- Organise groups
- Review the learning outcomes and skills
- Brainstorm ideas
- Focus on key information
- Have groups make decisions about content

2 Development

Project groups

Step 1: Assign roles and responsibilities

Step 2: Research and analyse

Step 3: Draft and review

- Put together work
- Peer-correct
- Express opinions and make choices

3 Production

Project groups

Step 1: Prepare

- Decide how the project will look and who will speak
- Practise

Step 2: Present

- Take turns presenting
- Ask questions and give feedback

Step 3: Reflect

- Discuss all stages of the process

Pre-evaluation (self-evaluation)

Tools for students:
KWL chart, My learning diary, Peer-evaluation form

Tools for teachers:
Teacher's evaluation form

> Evaluation tools pp67–70

Formative evaluation (self-evaluation, peer-evaluation, observation)

Tools for students:
KWL chart, My learning diary, graphic organisers, Peer-evaluation form

Tools for teachers:
Teacher's evaluation form

> Evaluation tools pp67–70

Formative and summative evaluation

Tools for students:
KWL chart, My learning diary, Peer-evaluation form

Tools for teachers:
Teacher's evaluation form, Evaluation rubric

> Evaluation tools pp67–70

> Evaluation rubric p21

Reflection (you and students)

1. Have *student-to-student*, *student-to-teacher* and *teacher-to-student* discussions on evaluation grades.

2. Identify areas for improvement in future projects using the Evaluation tools.

> Evaluation p20

L1 IN PROJECT WORK

Many teachers believe that the only way for students to learn English effectively is by using it at all times in class. They feel that any time students spend using their own language is a missed opportunity.

Do you allow L1 use in your classroom? If you do, don't worry: there is little data to support the above idea (Kerr, 2016)[1]. In fact, there are occasions when allowing students to use L1 is positive. This is particularly true of project work.

We can use L1 in different steps of the project cycle. Take *Clarifying the project* as an example (Preparation stage, Step 4). If students fail to understand the project's objectives, they won't carry it out properly. Allowing L1 use is not a 'missed opportunity' here. It ensures a richer project experience.

Of course, this doesn't mean you should use students' own language *all* of the time. You have to consider factors like age, level, the complexity of the project and its outcomes. The question is not *if* you should use own language, but *when*, *how* and *how much*.

At Level 4, we suggest you encourage the use of English for most stages of each project. This includes during in-depth discussions of the topic and reflection stages.

Tips for L1 use

- Set rules for when students can use L1.

- Encourage groups to monitor their own-language use and explore English equivalents.

- Allow students 'own-language moments' (Kerr, 2014: 26–29)[2], such as preparing for speaking activities. Remember that the students' goal is to produce English in the Production stage of project work.

OL = Own language, E = English, ▩ shows suggested language

THE LEARNING STAGES OF PROJECT WORK		
1 Preparation	OL	E
Introducing and discussing the topic		▩
Analysing the model for the project		▩
Going through the *How to* tips		▩
Clarifying the project		▩
2 Development	OL	E
Assigning roles and responsibilities		▩
Researching and analysing	▩	
Drafting and reviewing		▩
3 Production	OL	E
Preparing the final presentation	▩	
Presenting the project		▩
Reflecting on the process		▩

[1] Kerr, Philip (2016). 'The learner's own language.' *Explorations in English Language and Linguistics*. 3.1: 1–7.
[2] Kerr, Philip (2014). *Translation and Own-language Activities*. Cambridge: Cambridge University Press.

MIXED ABILITIES IN PROJECT WORK

How can you teach in ways that suit each type of learner? Projects offer a great advantage in this area, as students can explore different ways of completing them.

Mixed-ability classes can have individual differences such as motivation, ability, age and experience. Allow your students to express their ideas in different ways, and remember that no one will be happy with a project that is too difficult or too easy.

Studies have shown that adolescence is the best time for instructed language learning. Teenagers are faster at learning and are ready to observe and use rules (DeKeyser, 2010)[1]. Your activities should reflect this, which means getting to know your students and their differences in the following four areas:

Cognitive maturity
Your students' ages and experiences affect their ability to understand and follow instructions.

Adapt instructions according to level and avoid complicated words and phrases with beginners and elementary students.

Proficiency
Every member of your class will have a different language level.

Make sure tasks involve an appropriate degree of difficulty and are suitably challenging. Provide the levels of support needed.

Interests
Teenagers have a wide variety of interests and skills.

Allow students to take roles within a project that help them develop their personal interests and relate to the main task. Encourage them to expand their knowledge.

Learning preferences
Everyone has different learning preferences, such as reading, taking notes, asking questions, listening, moving around or watching videos.

Use a variety of learning styles in your classroom, such as visual, kinaesthetic, auditory, multimodal or text.

The roles of the facilitator

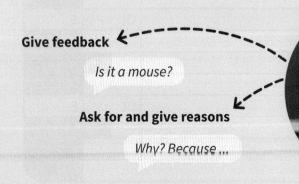

Give feedback
Is it a mouse?

Ask for and give reasons
Why? Because ...

Encourage participation
What do you think?

Listen actively
That's interesting! Really?

---

[1] DeKeyser, R., Alfi-Shabtay, I., & Ravid, D. (2010). 'Cross-linguistic evidence for the nature of age effects in second language acquisition.' *Applied Psycholinguistics*, 31(3), 413–438.

Classroom suggestions

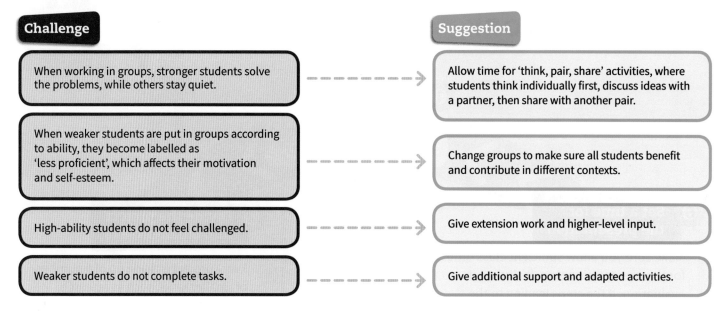

Challenge

| When working in groups, stronger students solve the problems, while others stay quiet. |

Suggestion

| Allow time for 'think, pair, share' activities, where students think individually first, discuss ideas with a partner, then share with another pair. |

| When weaker students are put in groups according to ability, they become labelled as 'less proficient', which affects their motivation and self-esteem. |

| Change groups to make sure all students benefit and contribute in different contexts. |

| High-ability students do not feel challenged. |

| Give extension work and higher-level input. |

| Weaker students do not complete tasks. |

| Give additional support and adapted activities. |

Differentiated instruction

We provide a specific suggestion for differentiated instruction in each project. Each one has three categories:

1 *Support* activities help students to better understand the tasks and concepts

2 *Consolidation* activities reinforce what students are learning

3 *Extension* activities provide additional challenges for more proficient students.

1 PREPARATION		
Support	**Consolidation**	**Extension**
Suggest ways to record and keep notes. Extend time limits. Give specific goals related to competencies.	Have students organise ideas. Provide specific tasks to improve competencies. Give extra roles and responsibilities.	Suggest alternative ideas. Focus on additional competencies. Set additional goals.

2 DEVELOPMENT		
Support	**Consolidation**	**Extension**
Provide more examples of models. Suggest sources for research. Give essential information that helps with students' roles. Ask specific questions about findings.	Analyse different models. Have students share opinions. Make additional notes of findings. Check sources. Give extra responsibility in line with roles.	Produce another model for the project. Analyse opinions. Look for different points of view. Allow for peer-teaching.

3 PRODUCTION		
Support	**Consolidation**	**Extension**
Check level-appropriate participation during presentation. Allow feedback in own language. Suggest ways to improve.	Encourage feedback in English. Have students discuss self-evaluation. Encourage suggestions for ways to improve.	Give all feedback and evaluation in English. Have students interview each other about what they learned. Encourage suggestions for ways to improve.

TIME MANAGEMENT IN PROJECT WORK

① Be prepared

Take a look at the project before you start the unit.

② Divide the project into smaller tasks

Every project is made up of a number of smaller tasks, such as research, preparation, organising notes and brainstorming. Ask yourself:

- *How long will each task take?*
- *Can the task be done in class or out of class?*
- *At what stage of the unit can students complete each step?*
- *What language do they need?*

By approaching the project this way, you will see that the steps may not take up too much class time.

⑥ Set a time for the presentation

Make sure you allow sufficient class time for the presentation step, including its evaluation. If the steps leading to the final product have been distributed and completed in an organised way, it's likely there will be more time for presenting it.

⑤ Be flexible between projects

How much time you give students for each task will vary from project to project. It may depend on factors such as previous knowledge, level of language difficulty or access to information.

③ Prioritise and set short-term goals

Think about how the project groups can best use class time. Should they brainstorm, draw pictures or organise sentences? Be clear about what you want the groups to achieve by the end of each session.

④ Help students plan out-of-class assignments

Ensure the groups understand that the out-of-class tasks are just as important as the in-class ones when preparing a project. Set goals and give time limits. Encourage them to use their My time-management plans when you see this icon: ⏰

> My time-management plan p71

It is important that groups present their projects when they expect to do so. It can be demotivating if you run out of time before they present.

CHALLENGES AND IMPLICATIONS

Students have had plenty of exposure to different learning styles through project work: visual, aural, verbal, physical and logical. Throughout secondary school, they have learned in groups and have also worked alone. The variety of projects in Level 4 allows students to continue developing their skills, no matter which learning style they prefer. As with previous levels, you can take advantage of these opportunities throughout the year.

Your students will be part of established social circles, but will be feeling the pressure of end-of-year exams and what they will need to do in the future. It is important to take these academic pressures into account.

What are some changes and challenges to expect?

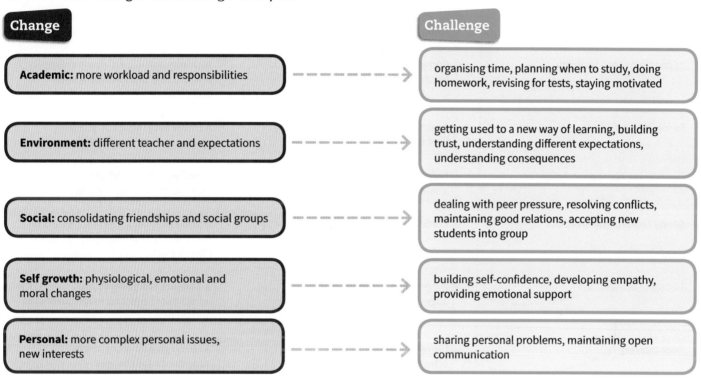

Change

Academic: more workload and responsibilities

Environment: different teacher and expectations

Social: consolidating friendships and social groups

Self growth: physiological, emotional and moral changes

Personal: more complex personal issues, new interests

Challenge

organising time, planning when to study, doing homework, revising for tests, staying motivated

getting used to a new way of learning, building trust, understanding different expectations, understanding consequences

dealing with peer pressure, resolving conflicts, maintaining good relations, accepting new students into group

building self-confidence, developing empathy, providing emotional support

sharing personal problems, maintaining open communication

All these changes and their challenges have implications for how to use project work in your classroom. You can encourage successful collaboration by:

- providing consistency in how you organise your classes

- explaining how much guidance you will give (less than previous levels), and detailing your expectations

- giving students autonomy about the ways in which they can work (using the internet, online programs, library, etc.) to encourage motivation

- observing group dynamics

- organising group work from the start

- making sure no one is isolated

- developing different skills through different ways of working (e.g. reflection, peer-evaluation, listening to others)

- continuing to pay attention to each student as an individual.

COLLABORATION

Collaborative skills	Behaviours	Level 4 Projects
Sharing resources	Helping group members to complete or improve work	**A fact file:** find and share online information; help each other find resources
Sharing tasks	Making sure all group members have a task and role	**A museum exhibition:** identify the main tasks and roles; divide the work fairly; set deadlines
Using social skills	Giving opinions, persuading, compromising, agreeing	**A poster:** agree on content; express opinions politely; ask questions
Encouraging responsibility	Completing tasks on time to finish a project together	**An infographic:** participate creatively; prepare own section; check each other's work
Resolving conflicts	Reaching a compromise and making final decisions	**A travel blog:** adapt or abandon proposals; listen respectfully
Disagreeing appropriately	Giving opinions politely to come to a solution	**A leaflet:** listen to different points of view; come to an agreement
Giving constructive feedback	Commenting on group members' work	**A presentation:** give compliments on and suggest improvements to each other's work
Listening actively	Responding to others' work or suggestions	**An advert storyboard:** plan information together; invite questions and opinions
Peer-tutoring	Correcting and editing each other's work	**A story:** give opinions; make suggestions for changes

Roles and responsibilities

Each project has specific roles; however, here are some general roles that you can apply at any time.

The **group leader** supervises, communicates with the teacher and manages participation.

The **resource manager** looks after resources and keeps the final product for presentation.

The **diary keeper** records decisions and tracks roles and responsibilities.

The **coordinator** tracks time and makes sure individuals complete their tasks.

The **inspector** checks and edits information.

The flipped classroom

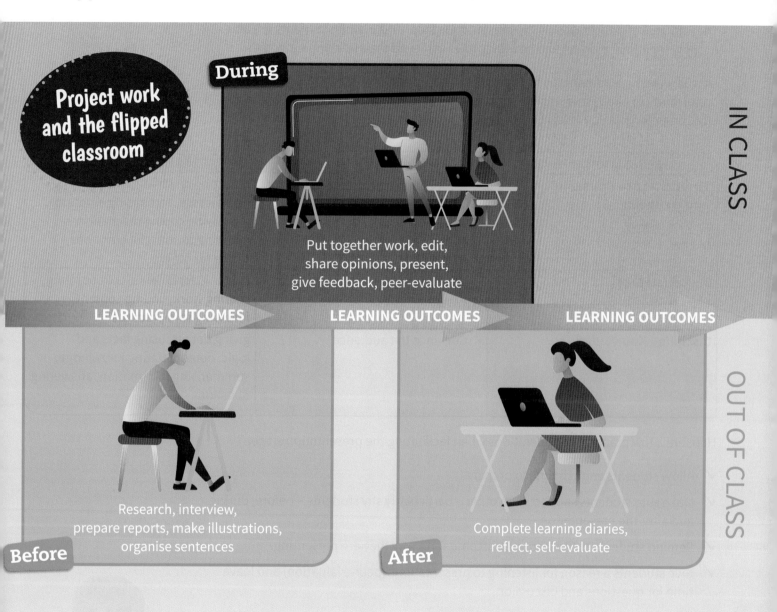

Project work and the flipped classroom

During

Put together work, edit, share opinions, present, give feedback, peer-evaluate

LEARNING OUTCOMES   LEARNING OUTCOMES   LEARNING OUTCOMES

IN CLASS

OUT OF CLASS

Research, interview, prepare reports, make illustrations, organise sentences

Before

Complete learning diaries, reflect, self-evaluate

After

Each project in this book contains at least one flipped classroom idea. Students are still collaborating when they use this approach. They have to share roles, get things ready on time, share information and resources and check one another's work. Students should plan out-of-class project work and use their My time-management plans. ▶ My time-management plan p71

How well did I collaborate?

At the end of the process, have students answer a few questions about how well they collaborated.

Did I ...
help my group?
share information?
do the tasks for my role?

Was I motivated?

Did we ...
trust each other in my group?
share opinions in my group?
share materials in my group?

What can I do to be a better group member?

PRESENTATION IDEAS

The end goal of project work is the presentation step. This is when students are able to show their final product and how they have achieved their learning outcomes.

As well as being a natural way to end the project process, this stage also gives you an opportunity to check students' progress in the foundational layers of the Cambridge Life Competencies Framework. 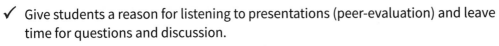 > Cambridge Life Competencies Framework p6

FOUNDATION LAYERS	ABILITIES	EXAMPLE ACTIONS
Emotional Development and Wellbeing	• Identify and understand emotions • Manage emotions • Empathise and build relationships	reflecting on strengths and weaknesses, verbalising emotions, employing coping mechanisms, adapting to stressful emotions, caring for others
Digital Literacy	• Use digital tools	creating documents, collaborating, sharing work, finding content, following safe practices
Discipline Knowledge	• Convince the audience	giving details, using facts and logic, demonstrating knowledge, summarising information, answering questions

Here are a few practical considerations when facilitating the presentation stage.

✓ Allow students enough time to prepare.

✓ Make sure students support each other – particularly shy students – before, during and after the presentation.

✓ Remind students of the learning outcomes and *why* they are presenting.

✓ Give students a reason for listening to presentations (peer-evaluation) and leave time for questions and discussion.

The following page gives ideas for ways to present some of the Level 4 projects. However, they are only suggestions. Where possible, let students choose modes of presentation that are most suitable for their projects and the classroom context.

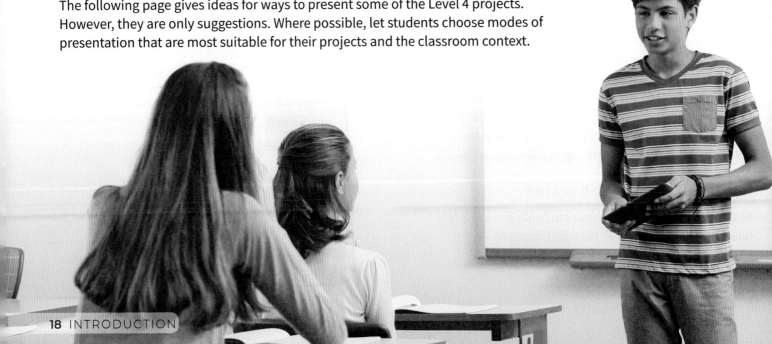

1 Booklets

1. **Write** the text and brainstorm images to use.

2. **Edit** and correct your work.

3. **Fold** two pieces of paper in half and staple them together.

4. **Decide** on a title and image for the front cover.

5. **Divide** the booklet into sections and decide on text for each page.

6. **Copy** the text into the booklet and add images.

2 Videos

1. **Make** a video or find images on a smartphone or tablet.

2. **Drag and drop** the video and/or images into the program.

3. **Add** effects and titles.

4. **Include** animations to move from one picture to another in interesting ways.

5. **Experiment** with other features, such as audio and special effects.

6. **Decide** on how to put the final video together.

Have students use a free video-making program to create their videos online.

3 Plays

1. **Choose** themes, characters and actions.
2. **Make** an outline of the sequence of events.
3. **Write** the script. Keep the dialogue short.
4. **Focus** on strong visual elements and add sound effects.
5. **Rehearse** and make necessary changes.
6. **Perform** the play!

EVALUATION

What?

Product

How well did students achieve their **learning outcomes**?

How well did they demonstrate these?

How did they **evaluate options** and make **decisions**?

Process

How well did students **plan** the product?

How well did students **develop** the project (roles and responsibilities, research and analysis)?

Did students develop **life competencies**?

Who?

| **Self-evaluation** | **Peer-evaluation** | **Teacher–student evaluation** |

When?

Preparation

After groups are formed: checking learning outcomes, brainstorming ideas, identifying key information, making decisions about content

Development

After each step: thinking about roles and responsibilities, researching and analysing findings, drafting and reviewing

Production

Before presentation: deciding on how to present

During presentation: practising presentation skills

After: giving feedback and self-evaluating

How?

Informal evaluation tools

KWL chart, My learning diary, Peer-evaluation form

> Evaluation tools pp67–69

Formal evaluation tools

Project evaluation rubrics, evaluation rubric, teacher's evaluation form

> Evaluation rubric p21

> Teacher's evaluation form p70

EVALUATION RUBRIC

The rubric below covers areas you can evaluate in every project. You can select some or all of these for each project when you feel it is necessary. There are also two project-specific rubrics with adapted evaluation descriptors in each unit.

Exceeds expectations (4): students show they are ready to go further and can take extra challenges in certain areas.

Very good (3): students complete the tasks successfully and as expected.

Good (2): students complete the tasks reasonably well with some things done better than others.

Needs improvement (1): students show room for improvement in most areas evaluated.

	4	3	2	1
Learning outcomes	Completes all stages to successfully achieve the overall learning outcomes.	Completes most stages effectively. Largely achieves overall learning outcomes.	Has missed some stages. Partially completes overall learning outcomes.	Hasn't successfully completed any of the stages. Overall learning outcomes unachieved.
Planning and organisation	Product is well organised, interesting and easy to follow. It follows the model for the project and no details are missing.	Product is well organised and easy to follow. Some details are incorrect or missing.	Product is similar to the model for the project, but is missing essential information. It follows the model with difficulty.	Product does not look or sound anything like the one specified in the task. There is little or no sequence to ideas.
Use of information and resources	Uses a wide range of resources to get information about the product.	Uses different resources to get information, with some gaps.	Most information is useful, but only comes from one or two resources.	There is little evidence of research and hasn't used appropriate resources.
Collaboration (Teamwork)	Collaborated in all stages and understood roles and responsibilities.	Collaborated in all stages and understood responsibilities. There was minor confusion about roles and responsibilities.	Collaborated in most stages, but there was some confusion about roles and responsibilities.	There was little or no collaboration throughout all stages. Didn't recognise roles and responsibilities.
Time management	Completed everything on time. Revised and corrected project.	Completed everything on time, with one or two steps at the last minute. Revised and corrected project.	Completed all steps but at the last minute. There was little time for revision or correction.	Did not finish project. Missed steps in the process.
Creativity	Product is very original and interesting. All ideas are well developed.	Product is interesting and very creative. Most ideas are well developed.	There is some evidence of creativity which could have been developed. Product is a mixture of original and copied ideas.	Little imagination or creativity. Most ideas copied and pasted from other sources.
Problem-solving skills	All group members participate and listen actively to solve problems effectively at all times.	Most group members are actively involved to solve most problems.	Some evidence of problem-solving but not by all group members.	Little or no evidence of problem-solving, either individually or in groups.
Language use	Excellent use of language. Project is clear and understandable with only a few mistakes.	Good use of language. Project is clear and understandable with some mistakes.	Adequate use of language. Project is understandable, but some sections need further explanation.	Random words are used in a confusing way. Project is almost impossible to understand.
Presentation skills	All group members participate. Presentation is well put-together and is clear and interesting throughout.	All group members participate. Presentation is mostly clear and interesting.	All group members participate, but the method of presentation is sometimes inappropriate or not engaging.	None of the group members fully participate. Inappropriate and uninteresting method of presentation.
Final product	Exceeds expectations.	Very good.	Good.	Needs improvement.

1 THE CULTURE PROJECT

A FACT FILE

- **Learning outcome:** make a fact file
- **Skills:** research information, decide on categories and sections, decide how to present information
- **Resources:** two or more fact files on aspects of culture, Fact file organiser p58, My time-management plan p71
- **Evaluation tools:** Project evaluation rubric p25, My learning diary p68, Peer-evaluation form p69, Teacher's evaluation form p70

 Unit 1

Before you start
Find two or three fact files on cultural topics (e.g. traditions, food, clothes, etc.) to show students in class.

Preparation

Step 1: Introduce the topic

- Introduce the topic of fact files after doing the vocabulary activities. p11

- Show students the fact files. Encourage them to say what the purpose of a fact file is and to describe what each fact file is about. Ask: *What information do the fact files show? What is each section about? Are there any images?*

- Discuss where we can find fact files (online, in newspapers or magazines, in leaflets and brochures, etc.). Explain that fact files present information about a topic in a clear way, usually using tables, bullet points and headings for different sections.

- Ask students to bring an example of a fact file (in English) about traditional dress or another cultural topic to the next class. Ask them to discuss how the information is presented.

Step 2: Analyse the model for the project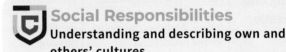

- Look at the model fact file with the class. Ask: *What is the fact file about? How is the information presented? What are the sections of the table? What do the images show?*

- Ask students to read the fact file and find two or three pieces of interesting information. Tell them to make questions with that information to ask a partner. For example, *What is a ghillie? What happened to people who wore Scottish dress after the Battle of Culloden?*

> **Social Responsibilities**
> **Understanding and describing own and others' cultures**
>
> Ask students to compare traditional Highland dress with traditional dress in their own culture. Ask students to say one or two things they like about traditional Highland dress.

Step 3: *How to* make a fact file Unit 1

- Go through the *How to* tips with the class. Ask them how they want to present their information (in print or digitally). Make sure students understand that their fact file will be about traditional dress from their own culture. Ask: *Where can you find information for your fact file? What information will you include?*

- Discuss using a video in a fact file. Ask students what free software they can use to make one or discuss finding a video online that they can show.

Step 4: Clarify the project Unit 1

- Follow the steps in > The learning stages of project work p10 .

- Brainstorm different types of traditional dress to include in the fact file.

- Ask groups to discuss what information they could research.

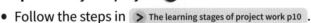

> My learning diary p68 **Preparation**

> Peer-evaluation form p69 **Preparation**

2 Development

Start this stage as soon as groups know their learning outcomes and what to research.

Step 1: Assign roles and responsibilities

- In project groups, students decide on general roles. **> Roles and responsibilities p16** Help them decide on further roles they can share.

- Explain that there are some important roles when making a fact file. Draw a diagram like this on the board:

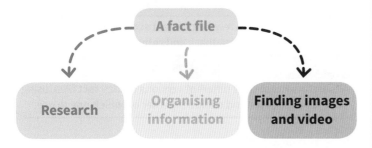

- Discuss the different tasks in making a fact file.

  Research: *Where can you find information about the topic? What sources will you use? How can you check the facts are correct? Who will decide on the most important or interesting details?*

  Organising information: *How will you present your information (tables, bullets, headings)? What sections will you have? Who will organise the information?*

  Finding images and video: *How will you make the fact file attractive? Where can you find images and who will select them? Will you use a video? Who will be responsible for it?*

- Encourage students to make notes and decide on roles.

Step 2: Research and analyse 🕐 Unit 1 ⏰ p71

⟳ Flipped classroom activity

Out of class: ask groups to do the first three points of the P L A N section in **Exercise 1** at home. Hand out a copy of the **> Fact file organiser p58** to each student.

In class: ask groups to discuss the information they found and complete the rest of the P L A N section. Remind students that the design of their fact files can differ from the model and the layout of the organisers.

Learning to Learn
Taking control of own learning

Learning to Learn
Taking control of own learning

Ask students how they are progressing with the out-of-class work in Step 2. Make sure that group members are using and sharing resources and allow more time if necessary.

🔄 *Own it!* learning tip

Sharing resources

Encourage group members to share where they have found useful information and online resources. This can include photos, maps, drawings and facts about the traditional dress they have been researching. If they are making a video presentation, ask them to share different ideas about which programs to use. Monitor and help with useful language: *Look at this resource. Why don't you try …? I've found lots of information at … .*

Step 3: Draft and review 🕐 Unit 1 ⏰ p71

⟳ Flipped classroom activity

Out of class: ask students to prepare their sections at home. Remind them to use the **present perfect simple** to talk about facts from unspecified times in the past and the **present perfect continuous** when the focus is on how long something lasts.

In class: ask group members to complete the P L A N section by checking each other's work. Encourage them to make suggestions for improvement. Finally, ask groups to put all their information together and make a draft of their fact file. If they are doing the project digitally, now is the time for them to insert videos and other media.

> My learning diary p68   Development

> Peer-evaluation form p69   Development

3 Production

Schedule presentation times and stick to them, checking that all groups present their fact files. Allow enough time for other groups to comment on different groups' fact files, ask questions and give feedback.

Before groups present their final fact files, check that they have followed and completed the steps, depending on which method of presentation they have chosen.

> Presentation ideas p19

As students complete their projects, check their abilities in the following Competencies.

Social Responsibilities
Understanding and describing own and others' cultures

Accepts others and shows respect for cultural difference.

Evidence: Students research historical reasons for traditional dress and why it is important today, and comment on each other's findings.

Makes informed comparisons between their own society and other societies.

Evidence: Groups think about similarities and differences between traditional clothes from different cultures.

Learning to Learn
Taking control of own learning

Identifies helpful resources for their learning.

Evidence: Students find and use different resources to help present their projects.

Finds sources of information and help (online and in school).

Evidence: Groups use different of sources to make sure facts and details are correct.

Step 1: Prepare ⟲ Unit 1 ⏱ p71

- Go through the PRESENT section in **Exercise 2**.

- As groups prepare their final fact files, ask: *Does the fact file contain correct information? Do the examples of the clothing in the images match the information in the text? Do you have any video? What else can you add?*

- Ask students to check their grammar and spelling, particularly their use of the **present perfect simple** and **present perfect continuous**. (See Differentiated instruction activities below for further practice.)

- Remind groups of the presentation date and how much time each group will have.

Differentiated instruction

Support
Help students decide what to include. Review the information in their organisers and make suggestions for how to present it.

Consolidation
Encourage students to rewrite different sections of their fact files based on their group's feedback and comments.

Extension
Allow students to draft different versions of their fact files (using tables, bullets, etc.) and decide together on which one to use.

Step 2: Present ⟲ Unit 1

- Draw attention to the CHECK section in **Exercise 3**. Tell the class to use these questions to check each group's fact files.

- Ask groups to present their fact files. As the class listens, tell them to make a note of two new things they learn.

- Ask students to discuss the most interesting facts. Encourage them to think about similarities and differences between the traditional clothes in the presentations and how they compare with traditional clothes in other cultures.

Step 3: Reflect ⟲ Unit 1

- After all the presentations, discuss the CHECK question in **Exercise 3**.

- Encourage students to think about each stage of the project process, including positive experiences and things they could improve. Ask: *How well did you work in your group? What did you find difficult/interesting? What new things have you learned? What would you change about your presentations?*

> Peer-evaluation form p69   **Production and Reflection**

⟲ Go to the digital collaboration space to set, track and assess students' work, or allow students to share and comment on their own work.

Project evaluation rubric: a fact file

Use these project-specific descriptors and your choice of descriptors from the **>** Evaluation rubric p21 to check students individually or in groups. Make your own evaluation form. **>** Teacher's evaluation form p70

	4	3	2	1
Creativity	Product is well organised with creative and interesting ideas. It is logical with very interesting facts. It uses a wide variety of images, video or other additional features to support information.	Product is organised with some creative and interesting ideas. It is logical with some interesting facts. It uses a variety of images, video or other additional features to support information.	Product is organised into some sections with a few creative and interesting ideas. It is logical but there are not many interesting facts. It uses a limited selection of images and additional features to support information.	Product is disorganised and lacks interesting ideas. It is not logical and has few interesting facts. There are no images or other additional features to support information.
Language use	Excellent use of grammar, punctuation and spelling. Excellent use of language from the unit (present perfect simple and continuous). Project communicates main ideas clearly with few or no mistakes.	Good use of grammar, punctuation and spelling. Good use of language from the unit (present perfect simple and continuous). Project communicates main ideas clearly but with some mistakes.	Adequate use of grammar, punctuation and spelling. Adequate use of language from the unit (present perfect simple and continuous). Project Is understandable, but some sections need further explanation.	Poor use of grammar, punctuation and spelling. Poor or no use of language from the unit (present perfect simple and continuous). Project is confusing, vague and almost impossible to understand.

 Cambridge Life Competencies Framework

You can also check students' progress in the following foundation layers.

FOUNDATION LAYERS	ABILITIES	ACTIONS
Digital Literacy	• Use digital tools	finding content on various websites, downloading images or videos, sharing work online, assessing online material, using video-making programs
Discipline Knowledge	• Convince the audience	presenting ideas, categorising information, giving facts and details, using appropriate video and images, answering questions

○ Flipped classroom activities

Evaluate

In project groups, ask students to discuss their completed Peer-evaluation forms and ways to work better as a group. **>** Peer-evaluation form p69

Out of class: Ask students to think about their progress at home. **>** My learning diary p68 Production

In class: Discuss what students have learned, using the information from their learning diaries.

> My learning diary p68 Production

2 THE HISTORY PROJECT

A RETRO MUSEUM EXHIBITION

- **Learning outcome:** make a retro museum exhibition
- **Skills:** research a period of history, organise the stages of a project (researching, drafting, checking and writing a final version)
- **Resources:** examples of history exhibits, History exhibition organiser p59, My time-management plan p71
- **Evaluation tools:** Project evaluation rubric p29, KWL chart p67, Peer-evaluation form p69, Teacher's evaluation form p70

Student's Book pp30–31

Before you start
Find two or three examples of museum exhibitions in brochures or online to show students in class. Make sure the examples include pictures and some text describing the exhibitions.

1 Preparation

Step 1: Introduce the topic
- Introduce the topic of museum exhibitions after completing the vocabulary and listening exercises.  p26
- Show students the examples of the exhibitions. Ask: *What can you see in the pictures? Where would you see these? What kind of information do people want to know about them? Why are these exhibitions important?*
- Ask: *What makes a good museum exhibition?* Then explain that good exhibitions provide information about artistic, cultural, scientific or historical objects in a clear way. This means they show information in an interesting way.
- Ask students to bring a picture of a museum exhibition to the next class and research some basic information about it. They can discuss which exhibitions they find most interesting and why.

Step 2: Analyse the model for the project 📖 pp30–31
- Students complete **Exercises 1** and **2**. Ask further questions: *What can you see in the pictures? How is fashion/technology/entertainment different today? Why would people find this interesting? What would they want to find out in the written text that goes with each object?*
- 🎧 2.13 For **Exercise 3**, ask students to give reasons for their ideas.
- Go through the information in the first column of the table. Allow time for students to complete the table and then check answers in pairs.

  Answers **3 technology:** Period: 1970s; Examples: computer on Apollo spaceships, computers in offices in companies; Changes over time: devices are smaller and faster, have more complicated displays and smaller buttons, people have computers at home; **music:** Period: 1970s and 1990s; Examples: record shops, record covers and artwork, CDs; Changes over time: music used to be sold as records in record shops, then CDs became more popular and now music is streamed or downloaded but records are also popular again.

- Ask students to find examples of the unit language in the texts: **used to**, **would**, the **past simple** and the **past perfect**.

Step 3: *How to* schedule 📖 p31
- Go through the *How to* tips in **Exercise 4** with the class. Agree on a final date for the project.
- Divide the class into their project groups to decide on times for each stage of the project.

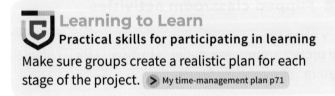

Learning to Learn
Practical skills for participating in learning
Make sure groups create a realistic plan for each stage of the project. **>** My time-management plan p71

Step 4: Clarify the project pp30–31

- Follow the steps in > The learning stages of project work p10 .

- Brainstorm periods of history and interesting areas to focus on from their own culture. Tell them they can use ideas from the box in **Exercise 5** in the PLAN section.

> KWL chart p67   **Know and Want to know**

> Peer-evaluation form p69   **Preparation**

② Development

Start this stage as soon as groups know their learning outcomes and have decided which period of history and which three areas to focus on.

Step 1: Assign roles and responsibilities

- In project groups, have students decide on the general roles. > Roles and responsibilities p16 Help them decide on further roles and responsibilities they can share.

- Explain that there are some important roles when creating a history exhibition. Draw a diagram like this on the board.

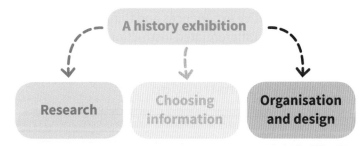

- Discuss the different tasks required to create a history exhibition.

  Research: *Where can you find information? How can you check the facts are correct? What sources will you use? Who will do the research?*

  Choosing information: *Which general information is most important? What areas are you focusing on? What are the supporting details? Who will decide what to include in the text labels?*

  Organisation and design: *How will you introduce the exhibition? What order will you put the information in? How will you make it interesting? What images will you use?*

- Encourage students to make notes and decide on roles.

Step 2: Research and analyse p31 🕐 p71

- Tell groups to decide who is going to research each exhibit and hand out a copy of the > History exhibit organiser p59 to each student.

○ Flipped classroom activity

Out of class: ask group members to follow the first stage in the *How to* schedule section at home. Tell them to research their exhibition using a variety of resources and add information about it to their History exhibition organisers. Ask them to include ideas for images.

In class: throughout the development stage, remind groups to stick to the schedule for each stage.
> My time-management plan p71 . Ask groups to compare and select information for the text labels and make notes in the second part of their organisers.

Step 3: Draft and review p31 🕐 p71

○ Flipped classroom activity

Out of class: ask group members to draft the text labels at home.

In class: students edit each other's drafts in class.

🛡 Collaboration
Taking personal responsibility for own contributions to a group task

Ask groups to make sure that everybody is aware of the schedule they agreed on for each stage and that each student completes their work as planned.

🔄 *Own it!* learning tip

Sharing tasks

After groups complete Steps 2 and 3, ask them if they have been following their schedules. Review the tasks students did to finish their projects and how they prioritised them. Ask if everyone was able to complete their tasks. Find out what happened if any area of the project went behind schedule.

> Peer-evaluation form p69   **Development**

③ Production

Schedule presentation times and stick to them. Tell students that the projects will be presented at the same time as a wall display. Allow them enough time to look at all the exhibits and ask questions and give feedback.

Before groups produce their final drafts, ask them to look at different examples of history exhibitions again. Help them with ideas of how to arrange their information and present it logically, for example, as a poster or leaflet.

> Presentation ideas p19

As students complete their projects, check their abilities in the following Competencies.

Learning to Learn
Practical skills for participating in learning

Produces a revision plan to focus on key skills and knowledge in a systematic way.

Evidence: Students check facts and give feedback on individual text labels within their groups.

Uses metacognitive strategies (e.g. time management) to maximise learning.

Evidence: Groups create and stick to realistic schedules.

Collaboration
Taking personal responsibility for own contributions to a group task

Follows the instructions for a task and alerts others when there are problems.

Evidence: Students check each other's progress within their groups to finish tasks on time.

Takes responsibility for completing tasks as part of a larger project.

Evidence: Students work alone in order to complete the larger task.

Step 1: Prepare 📖 p31 ⏰ p71

• Go through the PRESENT section in **Exercise 6**.

• Allow groups time to write and check final versions of their text labels and decide on the layout of their exhibition. Ask them to check the use of ***used to***, ***would***, the **past simple** and the **past perfect** and vocabulary from the unit.

• As groups prepare their final exhibits, ask: *Have you checked that the facts are correct? What images are you using? Do the texts match them? Is the design interesting? What can you do to improve it?*

• Remind groups of the presentation date and how much time each group will have.

Step 2: Present 📖 p31

• Groups display their exhibitions around the classroom.

• Ask the class to review the PRESENT section in **Exercise 6** and make notes about each area as they look at each other's work.

• Groups walk around the classroom and look at all of the exhibitions. Allow time for them to make notes about each one.

• Draw attention to the CHECK section in **Exercise 7**. Discuss the questions.

Step 3: Reflect 📖 p31

• After the feedback session, encourage students to think about each stage of the project process, including positive experiences and things they could improve. (See Differentiated instruction activities below for further practice.)

Differentiated instruction

Support
Students vote on the best exhibition and share the result with the class. Ask them to give reasons.
Consolidation
Pairs list the strong and weak things about one of the exhibitions and share the list with that group.
Extension
In their project groups, have students write three questions about facts from their exhibition. Then have two groups quiz each other.

> Peer-evaluation form p69   **Production and Reflection**

🖱 Go to the digital collaboration space to set, track and assess students' work, or allow students to share and comment on their own work.

Project evaluation rubric: a retro museum exhibition

Use these project-specific descriptors and your choice of descriptors from the > Evaluation rubric p21 to check students individually or in groups. Make your own evaluation form. > Teacher's evaluation form p70

	4	3	2	1
Creativity	Product is very attractive and interesting. Text labels have clear titles and information. It uses a variety of interesting photos. It contains accurate facts from a variety of reliable sources.	Product is attractive and interesting. Text labels have clear titles and some clear information. It uses some interesting photos. It contains accurate facts from a few sources.	Product is quite interesting, but it doesn't have a very attractive design. Text labels have some clear titles, but not all the information is clear. It uses a few interesting photos. It contains accurate facts but from only one source.	Product is uninteresting and unattractive. Text labels have unclear titles and not enough information. It doesn't have images. It contains facts from unreliable sources.
Language use	Excellent use of language from the unit (*used to, would*, past simple and past perfect). A wide range of vocabulary. Project communicates its main ideas clearly with few or no mistakes.	Good use of language from the unit (*used to, would*, past simple and past perfect). A range of vocabulary. Project communicates its main ideas clearly but with some mistakes.	Adequate use of language from the unit (*used to, would*, past simple and past perfect). Some vocabulary from the unit. Project communicates some of its main ideas clearly, but some sections need further explanation.	Product doesn't use language from the unit (*used to, would*, past simple and past perfect). Limited use of vocabulary. Project is confusing and almost impossible to understand.

 Cambridge Life Competencies Framework

You can also check students' progress in the following foundation layers.

FOUNDATION LAYERS	ABILITIES	ACTIONS
Emotional Development and Wellbeing	• Manage emotions	dealing with schedules, encouraging each other to complete the task, giving constructive feedback, responding to feedback respectfully
Discipline Knowledge	• Convince the audience	explaining exhibitions, giving details, summarising information, answering questions, talking about the past and how things have changed

↻ Flipped classroom activities

Evaluate

In project groups, have students discuss their completed Peer-evaluation forms and ways to work better as a group. > Peer-evaluation form p69

Out of class: Have students think about their progress at home. > KWL chart p67 Learned

In class: Discuss what students learned, using the information from their KWL charts. Ask: *What have you learned from this project?* Ask them to think about areas such as time management and sharing tasks.

> KWL chart p67 Learned

3 THE CULTURE PROJECT

A POSTER

- **Learning outcome:** make a poster
- **Skills:** research and select items of food, find and organise interesting information, decide on a design and select photos, maps and drawings
- **Resources:** two or more posters, Poster organiser p60, My time-management plan p71
- **Evaluation tools:** Project evaluation rubric p33, My learning diary p68, Peer-evaluation form p69, Teacher's evaluation form p70

 Unit 3

Before you start
Collect two or three posters about food to show students in class.

1 Preparation

Step 1: Introduce the topic

- Introduce the topic of posters after completing the reading exercises. p36 Ask: *How would you make a poster about different types of food? What information would you include?* Discuss ideas.

- Show students the food posters. Encourage them to say what area of food the posters focus on. Ask: *What interesting information do the posters have? How is the information presented?*

- Remind students that posters use both text and pictures to get people's attention. Ask: *Are the posters divided into different parts? What pictures can you see?*

- Ask students to bring a poster (or an image of a poster) containing factual information to the next class. Tell them that the posters should be in English. Ask them to discuss which posters are most attractive, and why.

Step 2: Analyse the model for the project ⬦ Unit 3

⟳ Flipped classroom activity

Out of class: ask students to read the model poster. Ask them to prepare ideas for these questions: *What are the most important ideas? What interesting facts are there? Are the pictures interesting? How is traditional Aboriginal food different from traditional food in your country?*

In class: ask students to discuss their ideas. Then ask students to find similarities and differences between the design of the model poster and the examples they brought to class. Ask: *Which ideas would you use for your own poster? Why?*

🛡 Creative Thinking
Creating new content from own ideas or other resources

Write the best ideas from the discussion in Step 2 on the board and tell students to make a note of the ideas they want to use in their own poster.

Step 3: *How to* design a poster ⬦ Unit 3

- Go through the *How to* tips with the class. Tell students that they will need a general title for their poster and then will organise the information about their area of food into different items of food.

- Discuss where students can find photos and why clear handwriting is important.

Step 4: Clarify the project ⬦ Unit 3

- Follow the steps in > **The learning stages of project work p10** .

- Brainstorm different areas of food to research. Write a list on the board, together with any interesting information students already know and where they can find out more.

- Tell groups to choose an area of food for their poster.

> **My learning diary p68** Preparation

> **Peer-evaluation form p69** Preparation

2 Development

Start this stage as soon as groups know their learning outcomes and have chosen an area of food for their poster.

Step 1: Assign roles and responsibilities

- In project groups, have students decide on general roles. **> Roles and responsibilities p16** Help them decide on further roles and responsibilities they can share.

- Explain that there are some important roles and responsibilities when making a poster. Draw a diagram like this on the board.

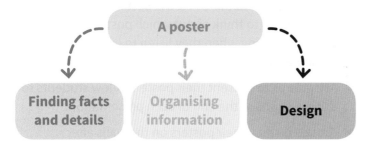

- Discuss the different tasks required to make a poster.

    Finding facts and details: *How will you decide on which foods to research? Where can you find information about them? How can you check this information is correct? What information will readers find interesting? Who will decide what information to include?*

    Organising information: *What information goes in the introduction? What information will you need about different foods? Who will be responsible for organising the information?*

    Design: *What can make the poster attractive? Where can you find photos? Do the photos match the information in the text? Who will select them?*

- Encourage students to make notes and share roles.

Step 2: Research and analyse Unit 3 🕐 p71

- Have groups start the PLAN section in **Exercise 1**. They discuss the area of food they have chosen and select five or six food items to concentrate on.

- Hand out a copy of the **> Poster organiser p60** to each student.

⏱ Flipped classroom activity

Out of class: ask students to find information to complete the organiser. Draw attention to the type of information they can look for in the second bullet of **Exercise 1**.

In class: students compare the information in their organisers and agree on which is the most interesting to include. Allow time for them to discuss the design of their poster and tell them to give a section for each group member to prepare.

Step 3: Draft and review Unit 3 p71

⏱ Flipped classroom activity

Out of class: ask students to prepare their sections at home. Remind them to find photos, maps and drawings.

In class: allow time for students to check and correct each other's work and create a first draft of the final poster. Ask them to concentrate on the vocabulary for each type of food. (See Differentiated instruction activities below for further practice.)

🛡 Critical Thinking
Synthesising ideas and information

Monitor students' ability to explore different ways of presenting the information effectively.

Differentiated instruction

Support
Help students check each other's sections. Point out areas which they can improve and ask them how they can do this.
Consolidation
Encourage students to use websites, dictionaries and their Student's Book to check grammar, vocabulary, punctuation and spelling.
Extension
Students make final decisions about corrections. They should explain their reasons to the group.

> My learning diary p68 Development

> Peer-evaluation form p69 Development

3 Production

Schedule presentation times and stick to them, so that all groups present their posters. Spread the presentations over a few classes, if necessary. Allow time for questions after each presentation.

Before groups produce their final drafts, ask them how they will present the information on their posters and give alternative ideas, such as a booklet.

> Presentation ideas p19

As students complete their projects, check their abilities in the following Competencies.

 Creative Thinking
Creating new content from own ideas or other resources

Responds imaginatively to contemporary events and ideas.

Evidence: Students research and choose an appropriate topic to focus on.

Makes an assignment original by changing the task or adding new angles.

Evidence: Posters have an interesting design and contain interesting and/or surprising information. Students present their ideas in formats other than a print poster.

 Critical Thinking
Synthesising ideas and information

Selects key points from diverse sources to create a new account.

Evidence: Groups use a variety of online or print resources to find interesting information.

Step 1: Prepare 🔖 Unit 3 ⏰ p71

- Go through the PRESENT section in **Exercise 2**.

- As groups prepare their final posters, ask: *Has your poster got photos, maps and drawings? Are you happy with the title? Is it short and interesting? Is the poster attractive? Does it have enough interesting facts?* Allow enough time for final changes.

- Encourage students to meet out of class to practise their presentation.

- Remind groups of the presentation date and how much time each group will have.

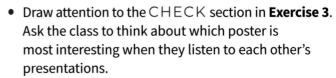
Own it! learning tip

Using social skills

As groups finish their posters in Step 1, encourage them to use polite language for expressing opinions, interrupting and making decisions, for example: *Let's ..., Excuse me ..., We could ..., Can I make a suggestion?, What about ...?, Why don't we ...?, Are there any more ideas?, Right, so we all agree.*

Step 2: Present 🔖 Unit 3

- Draw attention to the CHECK section in **Exercise 3**. Ask the class to think about which poster is most interesting when they listen to each other's presentations.

- Ask groups to present their posters. Allow students to ask questions at the end of each presentation.

- Groups display their posters on the walls after presenting.

Step 3: Reflect 🔖 Unit 3

- After all the presentations, discuss the CHECK questions in **Exercise 3**.

- Encourage students to think about each stage of the project process, including positive experiences and things they could improve. Ask: *Are you happy with your poster? Which section is your favourite? Which part of making a poster was the easiest/most difficult? What would you do differently in future? What have you learned from this project?*

> Peer-evaluation form p69   **Production and Reflection**

🔖 Go to the digital collaboration space to set, track and assess students' work, or allow students to share and comment on their own work.

Project evaluation rubric: a poster

Use these project-specific descriptors and your choice of descriptors from the **> Evaluation rubric p21** to check students individually or in groups. Make your own evaluation form. **> Teacher's evaluation form p70**

	4	3	2	1
Creativity	Product is well organised with creative and interesting ideas. It has a short and interesting title and includes the key information. It has an attractive design with interesting photos, maps and drawings.	Product is organised with interesting ideas. It has a short and interesting title and includes most of the key information. It has a fairly attractive design with interesting photos, maps and drawings.	Product is interesting, but lacks organisation. It has a title and includes some key information. It has a basic design with some photos, maps and drawings.	Product lacks interesting ideas and organisation. It is missing a title and/or key information. It has an unattractive design which is not related to the topic.
Language use	Excellent use of grammar, punctuation and spelling. Communicates its main ideas clearly with few or no mistakes.	Good use of grammar, punctuation and spelling. Communicates its main ideas clearly but with some mistakes.	Adequate use of grammar, punctuation and spelling. Communicates some of its main ideas clearly, but some sections need further explanation.	Poor use of grammar, punctuation and spelling. Confusing and almost impossible to understand.

 Cambridge Life Competencies Framework
You can also check students' progress in the following foundation layers.

FOUNDATION LAYERS	ABILITIES	ACTIONS
Discipline Knowledge	• Convince the audience	using persuasive language, giving specific details, providing interesting information and supporting details, answering questions
Emotional Development and Wellbeing	• Empathise and build relationships	helping others complete a task, using coping mechanisms when giving presentations, agreeing on content

⟳ Flipped classroom activities

Evaluate

In project groups, have students discuss their completed Peer-evaluation forms and ways to work better as a group. **> Peer-evaluation form p69**

Out of class: Ask students to think about their progress at home. **> My learning diary p68** **Production**

In class: Discuss what students learned, using the information from their learning diaries. Ask: *What new skills have you learned? How can your group work better in the next project?*

> My learning diary p68 **Production**

AN INFOGRAPHIC ON ANIMAL SENSES

- **Learning outcome:** make an infographic
- **Skills:** conduct research on animal senses, read articles, identify facts and opinions, use visuals to create an infographic
- **Resources:** two or more infographics about animals, Infographic organiser p61, My time-management plan p71
- **Evaluation tools:** Project evaluation rubric p37, KWL chart p67, Peer-evaluation form p69, Teacher's evaluation form p70

📖 Student's Book pp54–55

Before you start

Collect two or three different infographics (about animals or the natural world) to show students in class.

① Preparation

Step 1: Introduce the topic

- Introduce the topic of infographics after completing the vocabulary and listening exercises. 📖 p50 Ask: *What two words does 'infographic' come from?* ('information' + 'graphic') Explain that an infographic is a way of displaying information in a way that is easy to understand.

- Show students the infographics. Ask: *What is the topic of each infographic? How is the information presented? What images are used? Is the information clear?*

- Ask students to bring an example of an infographic to the next class. Ask students to discuss the infographics and how the information is presented.

Step 2: Analyse the model for the project 📖 pp54–55

- Complete **Exercises 1** and **2**. Discuss ideas as a class before allowing students time to read the infographic and check their answers.

  Answers **1** Africa and Asia **2** They use their trunks **3** Very strong, it has 100,000 muscles **4** For hearing and also to keep them cool

- **Ask:** *What is the infographic about? Are the text boxes clear? What information is in each? How are the facts presented?* Students can compare the model infographic to the examples they brought to class.

- Revise the language from the unit. Ask students to find examples of **modal verbs** in the model.

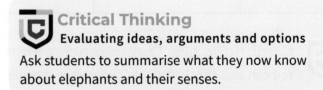

🛡 Critical Thinking
Evaluating ideas, arguments and options

Ask students to summarise what they now know about elephants and their senses.

Step 3: *How to* research 📖 p54

- Go through the tips in **Exercise 3**. Ask students to give reasons for why a tip is useful or not.

  Answers **3** 1, 2, 4, 5, 7

- Tell students that it is important to scan the infographic quickly. This means finding the most important facts and figures without reading the whole article.

- Check that students understand that when they make their infographics, they should use the tips in this *How to* section.

Step 4: Clarify the project 📖 pp54–55

- Follow the steps in > The learning stages of project work p10

- Discuss how different animals use their senses in different ways (for example, dogs using smell, bats using sound, etc.). Brainstorm a list of animals. Tell groups to choose one of the animals as a subject for their infographic.

  > KWL chart p67   **Know and Want to know**

  > Peer-evaluation form p69   **Preparation**

2 Development

Start this stage as soon as groups know their learning outcomes and have chosen an animal to focus on.

Step 1: Assign roles and responsibilities

- In project groups, have students decide on general roles. **> Roles and responsibilities p16** Help them decide on further roles they can share.

- Explain that there are some important roles and responsibilities when making an infographic. Draw a diagram like this on the board:

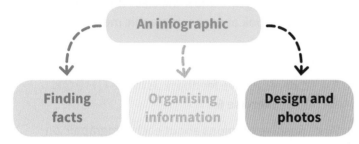

An infographic

Finding facts | Organising information | Design and photos

- Discuss the different tasks required to make an infographic.

    Finding facts: *What is special about your animal's senses? Where can you find information? How will you check that the information is correct? Who will decide what facts and figures to include?*

    Organising information: *Will you use general and specific information? How? What text boxes will you use? Who will be responsible for organising the information?*

    Design and photos: *How will the images make the infographic easier to understand? Do the images show the information in the text? Do you need any other pictures? Who will choose them?*

- Encourage students to make notes and decide on roles.

Step 2: Research and analyse 📖 p55 ⏰ p71

- Have students read the PLAN section in **Exercise 4** and choose senses for each member of their group to research.

- Hand out a copy of the **> Infographic organiser p61** to each student.

⟳ Flipped classroom activity

Out of class: ask students to research an animal sense and complete the first part of the organiser. Refer them to the correct tips in the *How to* section on p54. Remind them to check facts and figures using more than one source. Have them find images.

In class: ask group members to share their ideas and decide on headings, text sizes and the way they want to present information. Tell them to draw simple pictures in the second part of their organisers. (See Differentiated instruction activities below for further practice.)

Differentiated instruction

Support
Groups choose information and finish the design.
Consolidation
Allow students time to check information in their groups using other sources.
Extension
Students ask further questions and find additional information for their organisers.

🛡 Collaboration
Managing the sharing of tasks in a project

Monitor how students share work and how they choose information to use from each other's research.

Step 3: Draft and review 📖 p55 ⏰ p71

- Hand out a large piece of paper to each group. Students use the final ideas from their organisers to create a final version.

- Students add photos and pictures.

- Check groups are using language from the unit (such as **modal verbs** for obligation and necessity and vocabulary related to animal senses).

> Peer-evaluation form p69 Development

3 Production

Schedule presentation times and stick to them. Spread the presentations over a few classes, if necessary. Allow enough time for each presentation and for questions.

Before groups produce their final drafts, have them discuss different ways of presenting their infographic. Some groups may prefer to present their work digitally.

> Presentation ideas p19

As students complete their projects, check their abilities in the following Competencies.

Critical Thinking
Evaluating ideas, arguments and options

Distinguishes between fact and opinion.

Evidence: Students have chosen facts to include in their work.

Identifies evidence and its reliability.

Evidence: The infographic contains facts checked with a variety of sources.

Collaboration
Managing the sharing of tasks in a project

Works with others to plan and execute class projects.

Evidence: Individuals participate in research and design according to their roles.

Ensures that work is fairly divided among members in group activities.

Evidence: Groups have given one animal sense to each member.

Step 1: Prepare 📖 p55 ⏰ p71

- Go through the PRESENT section in **Exercise 5**.

- As groups prepare their final infographics, ask: *Are the facts correct? How do you know? What images are you using? Are they appropriate? Is your infographic easy to understand?*

- Remind groups of the presentation date and how much time each group will have.

Step 2: Present 📖 p55

- Draw attention to the CHECK section in **Exercise 6**. Ask the class to make notes about what they find interesting as they listen to each group's presentation.

- Have groups present their infographics. Tell each student to present the sense they prepared, but allow group members to help each other.

- Have the class ask questions at the end of each presentation.

- Ask groups to display their infographics on the walls after presenting and allow the class time to walk around and look at each infographic more closely.

Step 3: Reflect 📖 p55

- Ask students to give feedback as in the CHECK section in **Exercise 6**.

- Write positive opinions about each infographic on the board. Then have the class vote for the best infographic, saying why they found it the most interesting.

- Encourage students to think about each stage of the project, including positive experiences and things they could improve.

🔄 *Own it!* learning tip

Encouraging responsibility

Tell students that it is important to prepare their own sections on time so that their groups can check each other's work and finish the project in class. Remind group members of their general roles. Discuss any problems groups may be having in keeping to schedule. Discuss ways of solving any problems. Help students with useful language: *Why don't we …?, You could …, Let's try and …, Can you do that by …?*, etc.

> Peer-evaluation form p69 **Production and Reflection**

🔗 Go to the digital collaboration space to set, track and assess students' work, or allow students to share and comment on their own work.

Project evaluation rubric: an infographic

Use these project-specific descriptors and your choice of descriptors from the **> Evaluation rubric p21** to check students individually or in groups. Make your own evaluation form. **> Teacher's evaluation form p70**

	4	3	2	1
Creativity	Product contains detailed facts and figures. It has clear graphics that are easy to understand. It uses interesting images and a variety of text sizes.	Product contains some facts and figures. It has mostly clear graphics that are easy to understand. It uses interesting images and one or two text sizes.	Product contains a few facts. It has some clear graphics, but some are difficult to understand. It uses some interesting images and only one text size.	Product contains incorrect facts. It has graphics that are difficult to understand. It uses poor images and text which is difficult to read.
Language use	Excellent use of grammar, punctuation and spelling. Excellent use of language and vocabulary from the unit (modal verbs and animal senses). Project communicates main ideas clearly with few or no mistakes.	Good use of grammar, punctuation and spelling. Good use of language and vocabulary from the unit (modal verbs and animal senses). Project communicates main ideas clearly but with some mistakes.	Adequate use of grammar, punctuation and spelling. Adequate use of language and vocabulary from the unit (modal verbs and animal senses). Project communicates main ideas clearly, but some sections need further explanation.	Poor use of grammar, punctuation and spelling. Little language and vocabulary from the unit (modal verbs and animal senses). Project is confusing and almost impossible to understand.

Cambridge Life Competencies Framework

You can also check students' progress in the following foundation layers.

FOUNDATION LAYERS	ABILITIES	ACTIONS
Emotional Development and Wellbeing	• Empathise and build relationships	making decisions as a group, taking responsibility for own work, giving positive feedback
Discipline Knowledge	• Convince the audience	checking facts and figures, demonstrating knowledge, giving specific details, answering questions

⟳ Flipped classroom activities

Evaluate

In project groups, have students discuss their completed Peer-evaluation forms and ways to work better as a group. **> Peer-evaluation form p69**

Out of class: Have students think about their progress at home. **> KWL chart p67** **Learned**

In class: Discuss what students learned, using the information from their KWL charts. Ask: *Why are infographics useful? What do you like and dislike about them?*

> KWL chart p67 **Learned**

5 THE CULTURE PROJECT

A TRAVEL BLOG

- **Learning outcome:** write a travel blog
- **Skills:** research information about a region of India, choose interesting ideas, find maps, photos and drawings, prepare a section of a blog
- **Resources:** two or more travel blogs, Travel blog organiser p62, My time-management plan p71
- **Evaluation tools:** Project evaluation rubric p41, My learning diary p68, Peer-evaluation form p69, Teacher's evaluation form p70

Unit 5

Before you start

Find two or three travel blogs online to show students in class.

1 Preparation

Step 1: Introduce the topic

- Introduce the topic of travel blogs after doing the listening and vocabulary exercises. p62 Ask: *What kinds of texts do people create to share their travel experiences? What type of information do they show?*

- Show students the travel blogs. Ask: *What places are they about? Is the information in different parts? What images does the writer use? Would you like to go to these places?*

- Explain that a blog is a type of website, usually by one person, that presents information in a conversational style. Ask students if they read any blogs and why. Ask: *What topics can blogs be about?* Have students share examples.

- Ask students to find a blog about travel. They can discuss what the blogs contain in groups.

Step 2: Analyse the model for the project 🔍 Unit 5

- Students look at the sections, titles and pictures in the model blog. Ask: *Which place is this blog about? What information do you expect to find out about?*

- Ask students to read the blog. Ask: *How is the weather in Meghalaya? How does the writer travel around? What do people do there? What is the official language? What animals are there?*

- Ask: *Is the blog attractive? Is it easy to follow? Are you interested in visiting Meghalaya? Is the language of the blog formal or informal?* (See **Differentiated instruction** activities below for further practice.)

Differentiated instruction

Support
Students work in pairs. Ask them to make true/false sentences about the blog and test another pair.
Consolidation
Have students work in pairs. Tell them to underline the parts of the blog which give the writer's opinions and to circle any facts.
Extension
Tell students to imagine they are visiting Meghalaya. Ask them to agree on three things they are going to do and plan an itinerary.

Step 3: *How to* write a blog 🔍 Unit 5

- Go through the *How to* tips with the class. Ask different students to say why each tip is important.

- Make sure students understand that when they write their blogs, they should use the tips in this *How to* section.

Step 4: Clarify the project 🔍 Unit 5

- Follow the steps in ▶ The learning stages of project work p10 .

- Brainstorm the kinds of things which are important to include in a blog (local information, famous buildings, people, climate, opinions, etc.). Write ideas on the board.

▶ My learning diary p68 **Preparation**

▶ Peer-evaluation form p69 **Preparation**

2 Development

Start this stage as soon as groups know their learning outcomes and have decided what to include.

Step 1: Assign roles and responsibilities

- In project groups, have students decide on general roles. **Roles and responsibilities p16** Help them decide on further roles they can share.

- Explain that there are some important roles and responsibilities when writing a blog. Draw a diagram like this on the board.

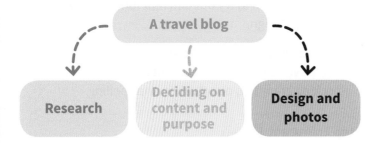

- Discuss the different tasks for making a travel blog.

  Research: *How will you find and check information? What will be the facts and opinions?*

  Deciding on content and purpose: *Who is your blog for? What will readers be interested in? What style of language will you use? How will you organise information?*

  Design and photos: *How can you make your blog look attractive? Where can you find images? Do the images match the information in the text? How will you make the blog (in print or online)?*

- Encourage students to make notes and decide on roles.

Step 2: Research and analyse Unit 5 p71

- Have groups start the PLAN section in **Exercise 1**. Allow time for students to research basic information about different areas of India before choosing one to write about.

- Groups decide on different areas to focus on. Have them discuss how they can write about different topics on different days of the blog.

- Groups decide what each person will write about. Tell them to decide on a series of activities and destinations for different days and give them days for each other to write about.

- Hand out a copy of the Travel blog organiser p62 to each student. Have them make notes about their day and check their information with their group. Have them decide on a title for their blog.

Creative Thinking
Participating in creative activities

Encourage students to use the information they find to help them imagine what it would be like to travel to their chosen area.

Step 3: Draft and review Unit 5 p71

○ Flipped classroom activity

Out of class: have group members prepare their day of the blog. Remind students to use friendly language, describe experiences and give both facts and opinions.

In class: have group members check each other's sections and then put their blog together. They can use maps and other information to check they are presenting events in a logical order.

Communication
Use appropriate language and register for context

Make sure students are writing their blogs with an appropriate informal style. Check that they are presenting personal opinions and using narrative tenses and not only describing a place.

> **My learning diary p68**   Development

🏠 *Own it!* learning tip

Resolving conflicts

Encourage students to try and agree when making final decisions about their blog. Have students listen respectfully and change their ideas if necessary, using polite language: *I think ..., Why don't we ...?, That's a good idea, but ..., What about ...?, Let's forget about that.*

> **Peer-evaluation form p69**   Development

③ Production

Schedule presentation times and stick to them, checking that all groups present their blogs. Spread the presentations over a few classes, if necessary. Allow enough time for each presentation and for questions.

Offer help and suggest ideas for how groups can complete their final versions successfully. Students may want to present their blog post digitally. If so, have groups work on the design and share their work using free online blog templates. If students are presenting digitally, they may want to include video.

> Presentation ideas p19

As students prepare and present their projects, check their abilities in the following Competencies.

Creative Thinking
Participating in creative activities

Encourages group members to make activities more original and imaginative.

Evidence: Students make content and design suggestions that attract readers' attention.

Participates in 'what if' thinking?

Evidence: Group members imagine what it would be like if they travelled to India.

Communication
Using appropriate language and register for context

Knows how to present points clearly and persuasively.

Evidence: Blogs give opinions and use clear language to describe experiences.

Uses language for effect.

Evidence: Blogs contain informal language and punctuation that express opinions in a friendly way.

Step 1: Prepare 🡒 Unit 5 ⏰ p71

- Go through the PRESENT section in **Exercise 2**.

- As groups prepare their project, remind them of the tasks they need to complete and the tips in the *How to* box. Tell them that they should be ready to answer questions about their blog entries.

⏱ Flipped classroom activity

Out of class: have students finish their blog entries at home, based on their group's comments. If they are presenting digitally, tell them to share tasks online. Encourage them to try out different fonts and colours in their blog design.

In class: ask groups to make any final changes to their blog. Have them focus on content and design before checking grammar, punctuation and spelling.

Step 2: Present 🡒 Unit 5

- Draw attention to the CHECK section in **Exercise 3**. Ask the class to think about these questions as they listen to each other's presentations.

- Groups present their blogs. Tell students to each present the entry they worked on. Remind speakers to look at their audience and ask for questions at the end of their presentation.

- Tell the class to make notes on what they like about each blog.

Step 3: Reflect 🡒 Unit 5

- After the presentations, discuss the CHECK questions in **Exercise 3**.

- Have the class discuss what they found interesting about each blog. Then hold a class vote on which regions of India they would like to visit. Encourage them to explain why.

- Encourage students to think about each stage of the project, including positive experiences and things they could improve.

> Peer-evaluation form p69   **Production and Reflection**

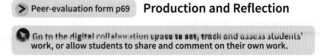
Go to the digital collaboration space to set, track and assess students' work, or allow students to share and comment on their own work.

Project evaluation rubric: a travel blog

Use these project-specific descriptors and your choice of descriptors from the **> Evaluation rubric p21** to check students individually or in groups. Make your own evaluation form. **> Teacher's evaluation form p70**

	4	3	2	1
Creativity	Product contains a wide variety of facts and opinions. Product has many interesting images and is interesting for the reader. It is very well organised and includes all the important details.	Product contains a variety of facts and opinions about the area. Product has some interesting images and is fairly interesting for the reader. It is well organised and includes most of the important details.	Product contains one or two facts and opinions about the area. Product contains images, but the content is not very interesting for the reader. It is organised in parts, but is missing several details.	Product does not contain facts or opinions about the area. It does not have any images and is uninteresting for the reader. It is disorganised and doesn't include any important details.
Language use	Excellent use of language to describe experiences and opinions. Uses punctuation very well. Project communicates its main ideas clearly with few or no mistakes.	Good use of language to describe experiences and opinions. Uses punctuation well. Project is understandable, but has some mistakes.	Adequate use of language to describe experiences and opinions. Uses some punctuation. Project is understandable, but some sections need further explanation.	Poor use of language to describe experiences and opinions. Contains mostly incorrect punctuation. Project is confusing and almost impossible to understand.

 Cambridge Life Competencies Framework
You can also check students' progress in the following foundation layers.

FOUNDATION LAYERS	ABILITIES	ACTIONS
Digital Literacy	• Use digital tools	finding content, checking information, creating a blog, collaborating and sharing work online, using digital presentation techniques
Discipline Knowledge	• Convince the audience	describing experiences, giving details, demonstrating knowledge, expressing facts and opinions, answering questions, using appropriate language and register

⟳ Flipped classroom activities

Evaluate

In project groups, have students discuss their completed Peer-evaluation forms and ways to work better as a group. **> Peer-evaluation form p69**

Out of class: Have students think about their progress at home. **> My learning diary p68** **Production**

In class: Discuss what students learned, using the information from their learning diaries. Ask: *What makes blogs interesting? How would you change your blog?*

> My learning diary p68 **Production**

6 THE CITIZENSHIP PROJECT

A LEAFLET

> - **Learning outcome:** make a leaflet
> - **Skills:** choose ideas, motivate yourself and others, design a leaflet with different sections
> - **Resources:** two or more leaflets on courses, Leaflet organiser p63, My time-management plan p71
> - **Evaluation tools:** Project evaluation rubric p45, KWL chart p67, Peer-evaluation form p69, Teacher's evaluation form p70
>
> Student's Book pp78–79

Before you start
Collect two or three leaflets on different courses to show students in class.

1 Preparation

Step 1: Introduce the topic

- Introduce the topic of leaflets after doing the reading exercises. p72

- Show students the leaflets. Have them discuss what courses they are about. Ask: *Who would read these leaflets? How is the information presented?*

- Explain that leaflets are short texts that give information and are colourful and interesting to look at. For example, they make people to do or buy something, tell them about an event or give advice. Ask students to say what leaflets they have seen recently.

- Have students bring a leaflet to the next class. Discuss each leaflet and what students like and dislike about them.

Step 2: Analyse the model for the project 📖 pp78–79

- 🎧 6.10 Complete **Exercises 1** to **3**. Play the audio and have students read along. Discuss answers for **Exercise 2** and ask students to point to the different features in the leaflet from **Exercise 3**.

Answers **1** a and d **2** **1** 14 to 18-year-olds **2** orienteering, building a fire, cooking outdoors; surfing, paddle boarding, scuba diving and white water rafting; rock climbing, abseiling, ropes course, parkour **3** Outdoor Survival Skills **4** No electronic devices **5** You can try something new and overcome fear.

- Ask questions about the leaflet, for example: *What sections can you see? What can you see in the photos? How does it make the reader feel?*

- Ask students to find examples of **conditional sentences** in the leaflet. Ask why the leaflet uses this language (to talk about possibilities and make the reader think about doing the courses).

Step 3: *How to* motivate yourself and your peers pp78–79

- 🎧 6.11 Go through sentences 1–4 in **Exercise 4**. Have students match them to sentences a–d and discuss why it is important to stay motivated while doing a project. Then play the audio and have students complete **Exercise 5**.

Answers **4** 1 d 2 a 3 b 4 c **5** 1, 3, 2, 4

- Ask: *What do you do to motivate yourself and others?* Have students share ideas.

> **Social Responsibilities**
> **Taking active roles including leadership**
> Discuss how the activities in the leaflet make people want to work together. Ask: *What leadership skills might you learn on this course?*

Step 4: Clarify the project 📖 pp78–79

- Follow the steps in > The learning stages of project work p10 . Explain to students that they are going to make a leaflet for courses that build teenagers' confidence.

- Brainstorm a list of possible courses for teenagers. Write ideas on the board.

- Discuss what resources students can use to find out about different types of courses.

> KWL chart p67   **Know and Want to know**

> Peer-evaluation form p69   **Preparation**

② Development

Start this stage as soon as groups know their learning outcomes and what resources to use.

Step 1: Assign roles and responsibilities

- In project groups, have students decide on general roles. **> Roles and responsibilities p16** Help them decide on further roles they can share.

- Explain that there are some important roles when making a leaflet. Draw a diagram like this on the board.

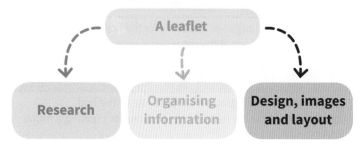

- Discuss the different tasks for creating a leaflet.

  Research: *Where will the course take place? Where can you find information? What can teenagers learn? What will they enjoy about the course?*

  Organising information: *What is the purpose of your leaflet? What sections will it have? What are the main and supporting details for each course? How will you present the information?*

  Design, images and layout: *What can make the leaflet attractive and easy to read? Where can you find images? Do the images match the information in the texts?*

- Encourage students to take notes and share roles.

Step 2: Research and analyse 📖 p79 ⏰ p71

- Have groups start the P L A N section in **Exercise 6** and choose two or three ideas to research.

- Tell groups to plan their leaflet. Remind them of the features in **Exercise 3** and tell them to use the model and other example leaflets for ideas.

- Hand out a copy of the **> Leaflet organiser p63** to each student to help them prepare.

⏲ Flipped classroom activity

Out of class: have students prepare their sections, using their organisers.

In class: have groups complete the feedback and correction activities from the P L A N section. Monitor and check that students are making positive suggestions for improvement. Have them make notes together on the *Conclusion* section of their organisers.

Step 3: Draft and review 📖 pp78–79 ⏰ p71

- Have groups put their information together to make their final leaflet. Remind them to think about the organisation of information in the model and what features it uses.

- Allow time for drafting and reviewing. Encourage students to use the **first conditional** to communicate with the reader.

Communication
Participating with appropriate confidence and clarity

Monitor progress of the tasks in Step 3 to check how well students make and agree on decisions together.

🏠 *Own it!* learning tip

Disagreeing appropriately

If students cannot agree on some of the items to include in their leaflets, encourage polite discussion. Have them make alternative suggestions to come to a solution all group members can agree with. Help with useful language, for example: *I'm not sure about ..., I don't agree because ..., Why don't we...?, How about ...?, Maybe we should ..., If I were you ... I'd ... .*

> Peer-evaluation form p69 Development

3 Production

Schedule presentation times and stick to them, so that all groups can present their leaflets. Spread the presentations over a few classes, if necessary. Allow enough time for each presentation and for questions.

Offer help and suggest ideas for how groups can make their leaflets (for example as a booklet).

> Presentation ideas p19

As students complete their projects, check their abilities in the following Competencies.

Social Responsibilities
Taking active roles including leadership

In group work, makes consultative decisions.

Evidence: Students work together to make final decisions on what to include in their leaflets.

Encourages others to participate and contribute in projects.

Evidence: Students encourage each other to work together using the ideas in the *How to* box on p78.

Communication
Participating with appropriate confidence and clarity

Starts and manages conversations with confidence.

Evidence: Groups discuss different parts of their leaflets in a clear and logical way.

Uses facial expressions and eye contact appropriately.

Evidence: Students look at the audience when giving their presentations.

Step 1: Prepare 📖 p79 ⏰ p71

- Go through the PRESENT section in **Exercise 7**.

- As groups prepare, monitor how they motivate each other. Remind them of the *How to* tips.

- Tell students to check their leaflets. Elicit or help them with phrases they can use to improve them.

- Check the language in the leaflets, especially the use of the **first conditional** to communicate directly with readers. (See Differentiated instruction activities below for further practice.)

- Remind groups of the presentation date and how much time each group will have.

Differentiated instruction

Support
Help students with the first conditional and other verb forms.
Consolidation
Tell students the language structure for the first conditional. Have them brainstorm different result clauses and choose the most interesting.
Extension
Students check their group members' use of the first conditional. Tell them to make suggestions for creating a more interesting message.

Step 2: Present 📖 p79

- Draw attention to the CHECK section in **Exercise 8**. Ask the class to think about this as they listen to the presentations.

- Have groups present their leaflets. Ask each student to present the course they worked on. Have groups give the introduction and conclusion to one speaker. Remind speakers to look at their audience and ask for questions at the end of their presentation.

- Check that students keep eye contact and show interest in what they are saying.

- Tell the class to make notes on what they like about each leaflet.

Step 3: Reflect 📖 p79

- After all the presentations, discuss which activities they would like to do from each other's leaflets.

- Encourage students to think about each stage of the project process, including positive experiences and things they could improve. Ask: *Were people persuaded by your activities?*

> Peer-evaluation form p69   **Production and Reflection**

Go to the digital collaboration space to set, track and assess students' work, or allow students to share and comment on their own work.

Project evaluation rubric: a leaflet

Use these project-specific descriptors and your choice of descriptors from the [> Evaluation rubric p21] to check students individually or in groups. Make your own evaluation form. [> Teacher's evaluation form p70]

	4	3	2	1
Creativity	Product is very informative and interesting. It is divided into clear sections with good images. It includes all of the features of a leaflet. All group members worked together.	Product is informative and interesting. It is divided into mostly clear sections with some good images. It includes most features of a leaflet. Most group members worked together.	Product is informative and interesting in parts. It is divided into sections with images, but these are not always clear or easy to follow. It includes some features of a leaflet. Only some group members worked together.	Product is not informative or interesting. It has unclear sections and no images. It includes none of the features of a leaflet. Members didn't work as a group and there was no creativity.
Language use	Excellent use of language from the unit (first conditional). Project communicates its main ideas clearly with few or no mistakes.	Good use of language from the unit (first conditional). Project communicates its main ideas clearly but with some mistakes.	Adequate use of language from the unit (first conditional). Project communicates some of its main ideas clearly, but some sections need further explanation.	Poor use of language from the unit (first conditional). Project is confusing and almost impossible to understand.

 Cambridge Life Competencies Framework

You can also check students' progress in the following foundation layers.

FOUNDATION LAYERS	ABILITIES	ACTIONS
Emotional Development and Wellbeing	• Empathise and build relationships	motivating yourself and peers, sharing roles, making decisions together, persuading and informing, making eye contact, using appropriate body language
Discipline Knowledge	• Convince the audience	talking about possibility, giving details, answering questions, presenting in a clear and logical manner, describing activities

⟳ Flipped classroom activities

Evaluate

In project groups, students discuss their completed Peer-evaluation forms and ways to work better as a group.
[> Peer-evaluation form p69]

Out of class: Have students think about their progress at home. [> KWL chart p67] **Learned**

In class: Discuss what students learned, using information from their KWL charts. Ask: *What phrases did you use to persuade people?* Ask them to make a note of any new language.

[> KWL chart p67] **Learned**

A PRESENTATION ON HOW TO BE HAPPY

- **Learning outcome:** give a presentation on how to be happy

- **Skills:** assign topic areas, make a mind map, select tips, find and prepare visuals, give a presentation

- **Resources:** two or more slideshow presentations, Presentation organiser p64, My time-management plan p71

- **Evaluation tools:** Project evaluation rubric p49, My learning diary p68, Peer-evaluation form p69, Teacher's evaluation form p70

 Unit 7

Before you start

Collect two or three different examples of online presentations to show students in class. If possible, find presentations that have a video of a speaker giving the talk using slides.

 Preparation

Step 1: Introduce the topic

- Introduce the topic of presentations after doing the vocabulary exercises 📖 p83, and after students have discussed the topic of happiness.

- Show students the presentation examples. Ask: *What is the purpose of the information? What will the presenter talk about? Who would give this type of presentation? How do the pictures help? What is the topic of each slide?* If any of the online examples you found have a video of the speaker giving the talk, first play them without sound and have students predict the content. Then play with the sound to check their ideas.

- Ask students to find an example of a presentation online and bring it to the next class. Tell them to look for a presentation on happiness or another emotion. Have them look at the presentations in groups and discuss how good they are.

Step 2: Analyse the model for the project Unit 7

- Have students read the model presentation. Point out that this is the script for the presentation and not what students should write. Ask: *How do the speakers present themselves? What six tips for happiness do they give? What information do they give about each tip?* Discuss the presentation's content.

- Get students' opinions on the presentation. Ask: *Do you think this is a good presentation? Is there enough information? Would you add anything?* Discuss what visuals the speakers could use to develop their ideas.

- Have students find examples of **gerunds** and **infinitives** in the presentation. (See Differentiated instruction activities below for further practice.)

Differentiated instruction

Support
Students list the six ways to be happy using gerunds: *Spending time with friends, being kind to others,* etc.

Consolidation
Students make sentences about each tip using infinitives of purpose: *Spend time with friends to make yourself feel better,* etc.

Extension
Students discuss how they could turn the tips in the model into an infographic or booklet for an audience.

 **Communication**
Managing conversations

Encourage students to use the information in the presentation while discussing the model and completing the Differentiated instruction activities.

Step 3: *How to* give a presentation Unit 7

- Go through the *How to* tips with the class. Have different students say why each tip is important.

- Discuss why it not good to read from a script *(you need to keep eye contact with the audience, answer questions, etc.).*

- Tell students that when they give their presentations, they should use the tips in this *How to* section.

Step 4: Clarify the project Unit 7

- Follow the steps in > The learning stages of project work p10 .

- Brainstorm with the class other ways to be happy. Write ideas on the board.

> My learning diary p68   **Preparation**

> Peer-evaluation form p69   **Preparation**

② Development

Start this stage as soon as groups know their learning outcomes and have brainstormed different ways to be happy.

Step 1: Assign roles and responsibilities

- In project groups, have students decide on general roles. > Roles and responsibilities p16 Help them decide on further roles they can share.

- Explain that there are some important roles when giving a presentation. Draw a diagram like this on the board.

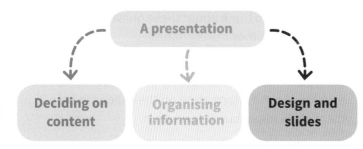

- Discuss the different tasks for giving a presentation.

  Deciding on content: *How will you decide on what makes people happy? What information can you give from personal experience to support your ideas? What information will listeners find interesting?*

  Organising information: *How will you put ideas into different sections? What is the most logical order for presenting your points? Are the points presented in a clear way?*

  Design and slides: *What pictures will you use? How will they support what you are saying? Who will be responsible for making the slides?*

- Encourage students to make notes and share roles.

Step 2: Research and analyse Unit 7 p71

- Have groups start the PLAN section in **Exercise 1**. Tell them to choose one or two areas each from their brainstormed list or the ideas in the first bullet point.

- Hand out a copy of the > Presentation organiser p64 to each student.

- Students complete the mind map in the first part of their organiser.

- Tell students to compare their ideas and choose what to include in their final presentation. Tell them to make notes as a group and decide on an order to present their points.

Step 3: Draft and review Unit 7 p71

○ Flipped classroom activity

Out of class: have group members prepare their sections, making notes in the second part of their organiser.

In class: have group members check each other's work. Allow time for them to prepare their slides. Help them decide which points to include and which are most important.

Social Responsibilities

Understanding personal responsibilities as part of a group and in society – including citizenship

Monitor students' ability to make choices in relation to happiness (diet, exercise, etc.) and to give examples of positive behaviour.

🔒 *Own it!* learning tip

Giving constructive feedback

Encourage students to give helpful feedback as they make choices about what to include in their presentations. Remind them to be positive about each other's ideas, identify things they think are weak and then suggest improvements. Help them with useful language, such as: *That's a good idea!, This works well., I'm not sure this works., I think we can make this better., Why don't you ...?, You could ... .*

> My learning diary p68   **Development**

> Peer-evaluation form p69   **Development**

3 Production

Schedule presentation times and stick to them, so that all groups give their presentations. Spread the presentations over a few classes, if necessary. Allow enough time for each presentation and for questions.

Allow groups time to finish their slides and help each other with any technical difficulties. Some groups may want to organise the ideas on their slides into a handout or booklet. **> Presentation ideas p19**

As students prepare and present their projects, check their abilities in the following Competencies.

 Communication
Managing conversations

Can use simple techniques to start, maintain and close conversations of various lengths.

Evidence: Groups follow the tips in the *How to* box when practising and giving feedback on their presentations and hold follow-up conversations on each other's tips.

Paraphrasing.

Evidence: Presenters re-phrase information on their slides and avoid reading the information aloud word for word.

Social Responsibilities
Understanding personal responsibilities as part of a group and in society – including citizenship

Is aware of positive behaviour in different groups.

Evidence: Groups identify and choose positive behaviours in relation to happiness.

Makes informed choices (e.g. in relation to diet, exercise, etc.).

Evidence: Groups make choices about what to include in their presentations, with information from their own experiences.

Step 1: Prepare Unit 7 p71

- Go through the PRESENT section in **Exercise 2**. Remind students that each group member will present their section.

- Allow time for groups to finish their presentations. Encourage positive and helpful feedback as they make their final decisions.

- Monitor to check that the slides are clear and organised in a logical order. Ask questions and make suggestions: *What does this mean? Would that be better here?*, etc.

- Remind groups of the presentation date and how much time each group will have.

- Allow groups time to practise their presentations. Refer them to the tips in the *How to* box.

Step 2: Present Unit 7

- Draw attention to the CHECK section in **Exercise 3**. Ask the class to think about these questions as they listen to each other's presentations.

- Remind speakers to look at their audience, speaking slowly and clearly, when giving their presentation. Tell them to use the information on their slides to help them show important information.

- Groups give their presentations. Tell the class to make notes as they listen.

- Allow time for questions at the end of each presentation.

Step 3: Reflect Unit 7

- After all the presentations, hold a class discussion on the CHECK questions in **Exercise 3**.

- Have the class find similarities and differences between their presentations. Ask: *What was the most interesting advice? Did any of the groups suggest something original? How clear were the presentations? How good were the slides?,* etc.

- Encourage students to think about each stage of the project process, including positive experiences and things they could improve.

> Peer-evaluation form p69   **Production and Reflection**

 Go to the digital collaboration space to set, track and assess students' work, or allow students to share and comment on their own work.

Project evaluation rubric: a presentation

Use these project-specific descriptors and your choice of descriptors from the `> Evaluation rubric p21` to check students individually or in groups. Make your own evaluation form. `> Teacher's evaluation form p70`

	4	3	2	1
Creativity	Product includes interesting and original tips related to happiness. It is supported by clear, interesting slides. It is logical and easy to understand.	Product includes some interesting and original tips related to happiness. It is supported by mostly clear, interesting slides. It is logical and fairly easy to understand.	Product includes tips related to happiness, but they are not interesting or original. It is supported by slides, although some are not clear. It is difficult to understand in parts.	Product does not include enough tips related to happiness. It doesn't have slides to support the information. It is illogical and impossible to understand.
Presentation skills	Speaks slowly, clearly and looks at the audience. Remembers what to say and paraphrases effectively. Keeps very good time. Answers questions effectively.	Speaks slowly, clearly and looks at the audience most of the time. Remembers what to say most of the time and paraphrases occasionally. Keeps good time. Answers most questions.	Speaks slowly, clearly and looks at the audience some of the time. Forgets some things and often reads from a script. Is slightly too slow or fast. Answers some questions.	Doesn't speak slowly or clearly and doesn't look at the audience. Reads everything from a script. Is too slow or fast. Is not able to answer questions.

Cambridge Life Competencies Framework

You can also check students' progress in the following foundation layers.

FOUNDATION LAYERS	ABILITIES	ACTIONS
Discipline Knowledge	• Use digital tools	using digital presentation techniques (e.g. PowerPoint), creating slides, finding images online
Emotional Development and Wellbeing	• Manage emotions	giving constructive feedback, reflecting on strengths and weaknesses, making choices, managing conversations, providing support and confidence, adapting to stressful situations (presenting)

⟳ Flipped classroom activities

Evaluate

In project groups, have students discuss their completed Peer-evaluation forms and ways to work better as a group. `> Peer-evaluation form p69`

Out of class: Have students think about their progress at home. `> My learning diary p68` **Production**

In class: Discuss what students learned, using the information from their learning diaries. Ask: *How confident do you now feel about presenting in front of groups?*

`> My learning diary p68` **Production**

AN ADVERT STORYBOARD

- **Learning outcome:** make an advert storyboard
- **Skills:** choose a product, list its features, create a storyboard, decide on a presentation format, give feedback
- **Resources:** two or more adverts for products, Advert storyboard organiser p65, My time-management plan p71
- **Evaluation tools:** Project evaluation rubric p53, KWL chart p67, Peer-evaluation form p69, Teacher's evaluation form p70

📖 Student's Book pp102–103

Before you start

Find two or three short online adverts for different products to show students in class.

① Preparation

Step 1: Introduce the topic

- Introduce the topic of adverts any time after doing the vocabulary activities. 📖 p95 Ask: *Where do you usually see adverts? What types of products do they advertise? What is a good advert?* Discuss ideas.

- Show students the online adverts. Encourage them to say what they are for and describe what is in each scene. Ask: *What is the purpose of the advert? Is it a good advert?*

- Remind students that adverts give information about products or places, usually to get people to buy or visit them.

- Ask students to bring an example of an advert (in English) about a product to the next class. Have them discuss the different scenes and the information they present and say whether the advert makes them want to buy the product and why.

Step 2: Analyse the model for the project 📖 pp102–103

- Complete **Exercise 1**. Discuss what is happening in the pictures and predict words that might be heard.

Answers 1 A backpack (Funpack)

- 🎧 8.10 Complete **Exercises 2** and **3**. Have students look at the pictures again and think of example dialogues for each. Ask: *What is the problem in this picture? What is the girl saying? What is special about the backpack?*, etc. Play the audio to check. Then play it again for students to write details in the table.

Answers 3 2 A Funpack 3 Waterproof, a charger pocket, personalised colours 4 Katia and her friend 5 Where to find the Funpack, special features 6 Packed full of fun!

- 🎧 8.10 Play the audio again and revise the language from the unit. Ask students to call out when they hear examples of **indefinite pronouns, reflexive pronouns, defining relative clauses** and **non-defining relative clauses**.

🛡️ **Critical Thinking**
Understanding and analysing links between ideas

Monitor students' ability to identify the important information from the advert. Ask them to decide whether they guessed the dialogue from the pictures.

Step 3: *How to* give feedback 📖 p102

- Go through the phrases in **Exercise 4** with the class. Have students take turns to call out answers.

Answers 4 1 best 2 positive 3 how 4 idea 5 maybe 6 work

- As you check students' answers, ask students why it is important to give feedback (so students can make changes to improve ideas). Encourage students to give useful feedback. Ask: *What is useful feedback? Are these phrases positive?*

Step 4: Clarify the project 📖 pp102–103

- Follow the steps in 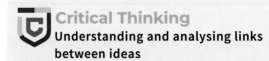 > **The learning stages of project work p10**.

- Have groups brainstorm possible products to advertise. Tell them their product can be anything of interest and they should bring their list of ideas to the next class.

> KWL chart p67 **Know and Want to know**

> Peer-evaluation form p69 **Preparation**

2 Development

Start this stage as soon as groups understand the learning outcomes and task and have a list of products to choose from.

Step 1: Assign roles and responsibilities

- In project groups, have students decide on and share the general roles. **> Roles and responsibilities p16** Help them decide on further roles they can share.

- Explain that there are some important roles when making an advert storyboard. Draw a diagram like this on the board.

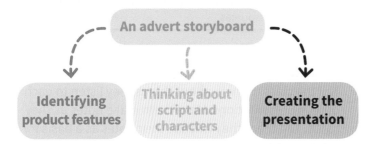

- Discuss the different tasks needed to create an advert storyboard.

  Identifying product features: *What makes people want to buy different products? What special features do they have? How can adverts focus on these features?*

  Thinking about script and characters: *Who advertises different types of products? What are they trying to do? What 'story' will the product have? What will characters say to each other?*

  Creating the presentation: *Who will create your storyboard? How many parts should it have? Does it need to be very well drawn? Does it need pictures at all? What descriptions do you need? What is the best way to present an advert storyboard?*

- Encourage students to make notes and decide on roles and responsibilities.

Step 2: Research and analyse p103 p71

- Have students start the PLAN section in **Exercise 5**. Tell them to choose a product from the box on page 103 or use their own ideas.

- Hand out a copy of the **> Advert storyboard organiser p65** to each student.

⟳ Flipped classroom activity

Out of class: have students complete the table in the first part of the organiser at home.

In class: have groups check their ideas together and decide what information and images to use. Then have them draw ideas or make notes in the second part of their organisers.

Step 3: Draft and review 📖 p103 ⏰ p71

⟳ Flipped classroom activity

Out of class: have students write a script for the advert at home.

In class: ask groups to check their ideas together. Make sure they are giving each other useful feedback. Have groups decide on the best mode of presentation for their advert storyboard. Hand out poster paper to each group and ask students to copy a final drawing and script onto it. If groups are not using drawings, have them write a description or act out their advert.

Allow time for groups to put a first draft of their advert together. Remind them to create a story from their notes and also agree on a slogan. Remind students to include examples of the unit language in their adverts where possible (**reflexive** and **indefinite pronouns**, **defining** and **non-defining relative clauses**).

Out of class: if groups are presenting their advert storyboard as a video or slide presentation, they can work on their drafts out of class (recording and sharing files, etc.).

🛡 Collaboration
Listening respectfully and responding constructively to others' contributions

Monitor groups' ability to give each other useful feedback as they put their adverts together. Tell them to make improvements to their work based on each other's ideas.

> Peer-evaluation form p69 Development

3 Production

Schedule presentation times and stick to them, so that all groups present their storyboards. Allow enough time for each presentation and for questions.

As groups work on their final drafts, share ideas about how best to present the advert storyboards.

> Presentation ideas p19

As students complete their projects, check their abilities in the following Competencies.

Critical Thinking
Understanding and analysing links between ideas

Distinguishes between main and supporting arguments.

Evidence: Students identify the most important features of their product and agree on what extra information to include in the adverts to sell it.

Identifies the basic structure of an argument.

Evidence: Students understand what the other groups' products are for and how they are useful.

Collaboration
Listening respectfully and responding constructively to each other's opinions

Listens to and acknowledges different points of view respectfully.

Evidence: Group members give each other motivating feedback while producing their final advert storyboards.

Evaluates contributions from other students with appropriate sensitivity.

Evidence: Groups listen and respond to feedback from other students after giving their presentations.

Step 1: Prepare 📖 pp102–103 ⏰ p71

- As groups prepare their final advert storyboard, ask questions. For example: *How are you going to present your storyboard? Have you got all the important information from your table? Have you focused on the special features of the product? What else can you add to make people want to buy your product?*

- Focus on **Exercise 6** in the PRESENT section. Make sure that students remember to use the information in Exercises 3 and 5. (See Differentiated instruction activities box for further practice.)

- Remind groups of the presentation date and how much time each group will have.

Differentiated instruction

Support
Help students decide the order of the information. Review their storyboard with them. Check it contains everything they need.
Consolidation
Encourage students to check each other's scripts for their sections. Encourage them to move text and information around.
Extension
Allow students to make final decisions on the order of information, script and mode of presentation. Ask them to find suitable online resources.

Step 2: Present 📖 p103

- Draw attention to the CHECK section in **Exercise 7**. Tell the class to think about this as they listen to each other's presentations. Have them make notes as they listen. Tell them they will use their notes as a basis for motivating feedback.

- Groups present their advert storyboards. If students are giving a poster or slide presentation, encourage them to each present one part of their storyboard.

Step 3: Reflect 📖 p103

- After all the presentations, hold a class discussion on which advert is their favourite. Ask students to give reasons for which advert was their favourite and to give motivating feedback.

- Encourage students to think about each stage of the project process, including positive experiences and things they could improve.

🏠 *Own it!* learning tip

Listening actively

When groups are sharing opinions about their storyboards, both during final preparation and in the feedback session, check that they are listening to each other's ideas and asking questions for more information or more details. Monitor to help with useful language, for example: *What do you mean?, Can you repeat that?, Can you explain?*

> Peer-evaluation form p69   **Production and Reflection**

🔖 Go to the digital collaboration space to set, track and assess students' work, or allow students to share and comment on their own work.

Project evaluation rubric: an advert storyboard

Use these project-specific descriptors and your choice of descriptors from the **> Evaluation rubric p21** to check students individually or in groups. Make your own evaluation form. **> Teacher's evaluation form p70**

	4	3	2	1
Creativity	Product is well organised with creative and interesting ideas. It has interesting images that focus on problems, solutions and special features. It uses interesting scripts and voiceover, tells a story and includes an excellent slogan.	Product is organised with some creative and interesting ideas. It has some interesting images with some focus on problems, solutions and special features. It uses scripts and voiceover, tells a story and includes a good slogan.	Product is mostly organised with a few interesting ideas. It has one or two attractive images with a little focus on problems, solutions and special features. It uses either scripts or voiceover and includes a slogan, but doesn't tell a story.	Product is disorganised and has no interesting ideas. It has no interesting images, and doesn't focus on problems, solutions, or special features. It contains a script with many errors, doesn't include a slogan and doesn't tell a story.
Presentation skills	Product information is presented in a logical and very clear order. Presentation method is appropriate (slides, video, acted out, etc.). Gives and responds to feedback very well.	Product information is presented in a mostly logical and clear order. Presentation method is mostly appropriate (slides, video, acted out, etc.). Gives and responds to feedback adequately.	Product information is partially presented in a logical order. Presentation method is occasionally appropriate (slides, video, acted out, etc.). Gives and responds to feedback adequately on some occasions.	Product information is not presented in a logical order. Presentation method is inappropriate. Does not give and respond to feedback adequately or appropriately.

 Cambridge Life Competencies Framework

You can also check students' progress in the following foundation layers.

FOUNDATION LAYERS	ABILITIES	ACTIONS
Digital Literacy	• Use digital tools	using tools such as video or slide presentations, sharing work online, recording scripts and voiceovers
Discipline Knowledge	• Convince the audience	writing an effective slogan, using persuasive language, presenting problems and solutions, telling an effective story

⟳ Flipped classroom activities

Evaluate

In project groups, have students discuss their completed Peer-evaluation forms and ways to work better as a group. **> Peer-evaluation form p69**

Out of class: Have students think about their progress at home. **> KWL chart p67** **Learned**

In class: Discuss what students learned, using the information from their KWL charts. Ask: *How did the feedback from your group members and others help you improve you project?* Discuss ideas.

> KWL chart p67 **Learned**

A TRADITIONAL STORY FROM YOUR CULTURE

- **Learning outcome:** write a traditional story from your culture
- **Skills:** choose a story, decide what information to include, sequence events and organise into paragraphs, use direct speech, illustrate the story
- **Resources:** two or more traditional stories, Story organiser p66, My time-management plan p71
- **Evaluation tools:** Project evaluation rubric p57, My learning diary p68, Peer-evaluation form p69, Teacher's evaluation form p70

   Unit 9

Before you start

Find two or three traditional stories from your culture to show students in class.

① Preparation

Step 1: Introduce the topic

- Introduce the topic of traditional stories after doing the reading exercises. 📖 p108 Ask: *What traditional stories do you know? Who told you them? When did you first read or hear them?*

- Show students the story examples. Ask: *Do you know these stories? What are they about? Why are they popular? What can we learn about our culture from them?*

- Tell students that traditional stories are stories that have been told for many years and that almost everyone in that culture knows. They include myths, folk tales, fairy tales and legends.

- Ask students to find examples of traditional stories in English. Have them discuss the plots, settings and characters in groups.

Step 2: Analyse the model for the project 🖱 Unit 9

- Have students read the title and look at the pictures. Ask: *Which place is this legend from? What do you think it is about?* Then have students read the story.

- Check comprehension. Ask: *Where is Mousehole? When did the story take place? What was the problem? Who was Tom Bawcock? What did he do? What happened?*

- Ask questions about how the information in the story is presented: *What comes first?* (time and place, background information) *What comes next?* (the story, problem and solution) *How does the legend end?* (Why it is culturally important today.) (See Differentiated instruction activities below for further practice.)

- Have students find examples of **direct speech** in the model.

Differentiated instruction

Support
Students work in pairs. Ask them to make a chart about the time, place and characters in the legend.

Consolidation
Students make notes about the legend in a story map. Then have them summarise the story to a partner.

Extension
Students make notes about the legend in a story map. They then write comprehension questions to ask a partner.

Learning to Learn
Practical skills for participating in learning

Make sure that students organise their notes well when thinking about the model.

Step 3: *How to* write a story Unit 9

- Go through the *How to* tips with the class. Ask different students to say why each tip is important.

- Refer to the model and ask students to find evidence of how it follows the first few tips. Draw attention to the organisation of the legend and how it starts and finishes.

- Check that students understand that when they write their stories, they should use the tips in this *How to* section.

Step 4: Clarify the project **Unit 9**

- Follow the steps in > **The learning stages of project work p10** .

- Ask students to brainstorm a list of traditional stories from their culture.

- Tell students that for this project, they will work in pairs.

> **My learning diary p68**   **Preparation**

> **Peer-evaluation form p69**   **Preparation**

2 Development

Start this stage as soon as groups know their learning outcomes and have discussed different stories.

Step 1: Assign roles and responsibilities

- Have students decide on general roles. Remind them that as they are working in pairs, they will need to take on more responsibilities. > **Roles and responsibilities p16** Help them decide on further roles and responsibilities they can share.

- Explain that there are some important roles when writing a story. Draw a diagram like this on the board.

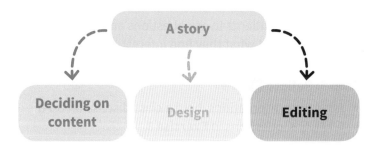

- Discuss the different tasks needed to write a story.

  Deciding on content: *How will you organise your notes for the story? What information will you include? In what order do the events happen? Who will write the text? What is the title?*

  Design: *How can you make your story interesting? Where can you find pictures? Do the pictures match the information in the story? Who will choose them?*

  Editing: *What resources can you use to check grammar, punctuation and spelling? Who will do this?*

Step 2: Research and analyse Unit 9 ⏱ p71

- Have pairs start the P L A N section in **Exercise 1**. Ask them to choose a story to write.

- Pairs make notes about their story. Hand out a copy of the > **Story organiser p66** to each student.

⟳ Flipped classroom activity

Out of class: have students complete their story organisers at home. Tell them to make notes in every section and include as much information as they can.

In class: ask pairs to compare notes. Have them agree on the order of events in the story and what each character says. Then ask them to decide who will write the story.

Step 3: Draft and review Unit 9 ⏱ p71

⟳ Flipped classroom activity

Out of class: ask the students who have the task of writing to write the first draft of the story at home. Then have them give the story to their partner to check. Remind them to focus on paragraph organisation, grammar, punctuation (especially around examples of direct speech) and spelling. Have both students find appropriate pictures that help tell the story or give information about setting, character or events.

In class: if necessary, have pairs rewrite parts of the story together. Then repeat the above process in class with their second drafts.

🛡 Creative Thinking
Creating new content from own ideas or other resources

Encourage students to be creative when retelling the stories. Have them focus on interesting events and how the story is culturally important today.

🏠 *Own it!* learning tip

Peer-tutoring

Monitor pairs as they edit each other's work. Explain that this includes checking spelling, punctuation and language as well as checking that the story is presented in a logical order with appropriate images. Encourage students to suggest improvements to each other's work and to make changes where necessary.

> **My learning diary p68**   **Development**

> **Peer-evaluation form p69**   **Development**

3 Production

Schedule presentation times and stick to them, so that all pairs either read their stories aloud or display them for the class to read. Spread the presentations over a few classes, if necessary. Allow enough time for each presentation and for questions.

Offer help and suggest ideas for how groups can present their stories (for example as a booklet).

> Presentation ideas p19

As students prepare and present their projects, check their abilities in the following Competencies.

Learning to Learn
Practical skills for participating in learning

Organises notes systematically.

Evidence: Pairs use the **> Story organiser p66** to make notes in a logical way.

Uses notes to construct original output.

Evidence: Pairs develop the notes from their organisers into an illustrated traditional story.

Creative Thinking
Creating new content from own ideas or other resources

Writes or tells an original story given prompts or without prompts.

Evidence: Pairs use their own ideas to tell stories as well as using other source materials.

Communicates personal response to creative work from literature.

Evidence: Pairs make their own suggestions about why the story is culturally important today.

Step 1: Prepare ◉ Unit 9 ◷ p71

- Go through the PRESENT section in **Exercise 2**.

- As groups prepare their final stories, remind them of what they need to include by referring them to the *How to* section. Tell them that they should be ready to answer questions about their stories.

- Have pairs make final corrections. Tell them to focus on spelling, punctuation and grammar.

- Make sure students include examples of **direct speech** in their stories.

- If students are going to be producing their stories for others to read, make sure their handwriting is clear.

Step 2: Present ◉ Unit 9

- Draw attention to the CHECK section in **Exercise 3**. Ask the class to think about these questions as they read or listen to each other's stories. Tell them to make notes.

- If there is time, ask pairs to read their stories to the class. If there is no time for presentations, ask pairs to pass the stories around for each other to read.

- Encourage students to ask questions about each story and talk about what they find interesting.

Step 3: Reflect ◉ Unit 9

- After the presentations, hold a class discussion on the CHECK questions in **Exercise 3**.

- Ask the class to discuss what they liked best about the stories. Ask: *How was the information presented? Were the stories easy to follow? Why is each story important to our culture?* Then hold a class vote on the best story.

- Encourage students to think about each stage of the project process, including positive experiences and things they could improve.

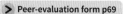 > Peer-evaluation form p69   **Production and Reflection**

◉ Go to the digital collaboration space to set, track and assess students' work, or allow students to share and comment on their own work.

Project evaluation rubric: a story

Use these project-specific descriptors and your choice of descriptors from the **> Evaluation rubric p21** to check students individually or in groups. Make your own evaluation form. **> Teacher's evaluation form p70**

	4	3	2	1
Creativity	Product is very well organised and easy to follow. Story contains all of the information highlighted on the organiser. It contains good ideas that make the story about the present day. It uses excellent images to help understanding.	Product is well organised and quite easy to follow. Story contains most of the information highlighted on the organiser. It contains some ideas that make the story about the present day. It uses good images to help understanding.	Product is organised in parts, but is sometimes difficult to follow. Story contains some of the information highlighted on the organiser. It contains one or two ideas that make the story about the present day. It uses images, but they are not always relevant.	Product is disorganised and difficult to follow. Organisers were not used effectively to plan information. It does not contain any ideas that make the story about the present day. It contains no images.
Language use	Excellent use of grammar and punctuation from the unit (direct speech). Project communicates its main ideas clearly with few or no mistakes.	Good use of grammar and punctuation from the unit (direct speech). Project communicates its main ideas clearly but with some mistakes.	Adequate use of grammar and punctuation from the unit (direct speech). Project communicates some of its main ideas clearly, but some sections need further explanation.	Poor or no use of grammar and punctuation from the unit (direct speech). Project is confusing and poorly written.

 Cambridge Life Competencies Framework
You can also check students' progress in the following foundation layers.

FOUNDATION LAYERS	ABILITIES	ACTIONS
Emotional Development and Wellbeing	• Empathise and build relationships	assigning roles and responsibilities, collaborating and sharing work, reflecting on strengths and weaknesses, peer-tutoring
Discipline Knowledge	• Convince the audience	telling an interesting story, giving details about plot, setting and characters, describing events, relating the story to the present day, answering questions

↻ Flipped classroom activities

Evaluate

In project groups, have students discuss their completed Peer-evaluation forms and ways to work better as a group. **> Peer-evaluation form p69**

Out of class: Have students think about their progress at home. **> My learning diary p68** **Production**

In class: Discuss what students learned, using the information from their learning diaries. Ask: *What techniques helped you write the story? Did you enjoy writing a story?*

> My learning diary p68 **Production**

FACT FILE ORGANISER

Type of traditional dress: _____

Type of clothes	Material	Other information

History

Images, video, other features

© Cambridge University Press 2020 Unit 1 Fact file organiser

HISTORY EXHIBITION ORGANISER

Period of history: _____

	1	2	3
Area			
Examples			
Changes over time			

Ideas for photos	**Drawing of exhibition layout**
Resources	

 © Cambridge University Press 2020 Unit 2 History exhibition organiser

POSTER ORGANISER

Title: _____

General background

Food	Food	Food
Information	**Information**	**Information**

Food	Food	Food
Information	**Information**	**Information**

Ideas for images (photos, maps, drawings, etc.)

INFOGRAPHIC ORGANISER

Title: _____

Species:	**What is the animal sense?**
Males (size, weight, etc.):	**What is it used for:**
Females (size, weight, etc.):	**Strengths or weaknesses:**
Lifespan:	**Special abilities:**
Interesting information:	**Any other facts:**

Images, icons to use

Infographic sketch

TRAVEL BLOG ORGANISER

Area of India	
Population	
Languages	
Geographical features	
Wildlife	
Famous buildings	
Famous people	
Climate	

Information about your day

Description of what you did	
Description of what you saw	
Feelings	
Weather	
Transport	
Other details (what was surprising, interesting, etc.)	

LEAFLET ORGANISER

Title: _____

Introduction

Types of activities for your course

Image ideas

Interesting language
(reasons for doing course, what students will learn/enjoy, etc.)

Conclusion

PRESENTATION ORGANISER

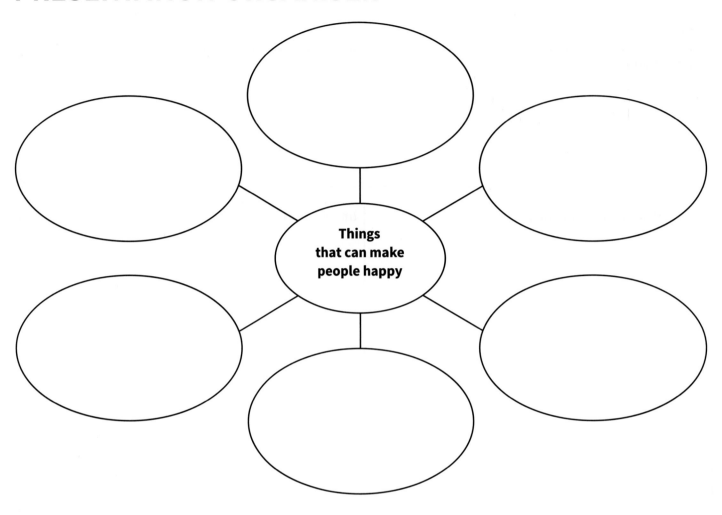

Things that can make people happy

Points to include about tip:	Main points for slide:
Supporting evidence from experience:	
Notes for your presentation:	**Ideas for images:**

ADVERT STORYBOARD ORGANISER

Advert features	Example
What's the problem?	
What's the solution?	
What are the special features of the product?	
Who are the characters in the story?	
What information does the narrator give?	
What's the slogan?	

Scene 1	Scene 2
Script:	Script:

Scene 3	Scene 4
Script:	Script:

STORY ORGANISER

Title: _____

Setting	Characters

Events

Beginning (include problem)	Middle (what happens)	End (solution)

Examples of language (direct speech)

Conclusion (how the story is important for the present day)

Unit, topic and project: _____

KWL CHART

Know	Want to know	Learned (Know now)
What do we know about the topic?	*What do we want to know about the topic?*	*What do we know now about the topic?*
		What do we know now about the tasks?
What are our tasks?		*What can we do now as a group?*

© Cambridge University Press 2020 Evaluation tools: KWL chart

Name: _____

Date: _____

Unit, topic and project: _____

MY LEARNING DIARY

1 PREPARATION
- What am I learning?   • What can I use? (for example, the internet, the library, magazines, …)
- Who is in my project group?   • What is my role in the group?

2 DEVELOPMENT
- What is difficult about this project?   • Who or what can help me?   • What do I like / don't I like?
- How can we make our work better?

3 PRODUCTION
- Is it a good presentation? Why / Why not?   • In the presentation, what is my role?
- How do I feel when I give a presentation?

Name: ....

Date: ....

Unit, topic and project: ....

PEER-EVALUATION FORM

1 In your group, think about your performance. Mark (✓) the columns.

1 PREPARATION	☺	😐	☹
We listen to the instructions.			
We understand the project.			

2 DEVELOPMENT	☺	😐	☹
We do our best in the project.			
We work well as a group.			

3 PRODUCTION	☺	😐	☹
We answer questions about our work.			
We ask questions about others' work.			

REFLECT

2 Write one good thing about this project.

....

....

....

....

3 How can your group work better in the next project? Write one idea.

....

....

....

....

Name: _____

Date: _____

Unit, topic and project: _____

TEACHER'S EVALUATION FORM

Group or individual performance grades for the selected ✓ general areas.
Grades are as follows: 4 = Exceeds expectations, 3 = Very good, 2 = Good, 1 = Needs improvement.

✓	Areas / Outcomes	Grade	✓	Areas / Outcomes	Grade
	Learning outcomes			Creativity	
	Planning and organisation			Problem-solving skills	
	Use of information and resources			Language use	
	Collaboration (Teamwork)			Presentation skills	
	Time management			Final product	

Group or individual performance grades for the project-specific areas.
Grades are as follows: 4 = Exceeds expectations, 3 = Very good, 2 = Good, 1 = Needs improvement.

Project-specific area	Grade
1	
2	
3	
4	
5	

🛡 Cambridge Life Competencies Framework

[Student's name / Group] _____ showed (✓) did not show (✗)
development in the following competencies and skills during this project.

Competency 1	✓ / ✗	Foundation layers	✓ / ✗
		Emotional Development and Wellbeing	
		Digital Literacy	
Competency 2	✓ / ✗	Discipline Knowledge	
		Comments:	
Comments:			

Overall grade: _____

General comments:

Area(s) of improvement:

Name: _____

Date: _____

Unit, topic and project: _____

MY TIME-MANAGEMENT PLAN

What tasks do you need to do for each step? Write them below and write the time prediction. Then tick (✓) each task as you complete it and write the actual time it takes.

Research and analyse

What do I need to do?		Time prediction		Actual time
1 ☐ _____	→ ⏰	_____	→ ⏰	_____
2 ☐ _____	→ ⏰	_____	→ ⏰	_____
3 ☐ _____	→ ⏰	_____	→ ⏰	_____

Draft and review

What do I need to do?		Time prediction		Actual time
1 ☐ _____	→ ⏰	_____	→ ⏰	_____
2 ☐ _____	→ ⏰	_____	→ ⏰	_____
3 ☐ _____	→ ⏰	_____	→ ⏰	_____

Prepare

What do I need to do?		Time prediction		Actual time
1 ☐ _____	→ ⏰	_____	→ ⏰	_____
2 ☐ _____	→ ⏰	_____	→ ⏰	_____
3 ☐ _____	→ ⏰	_____	→ ⏰	_____

Reflect

Answer the questions.

- I manage my time well during my project work.   ☐ Yes.   ☐ Can be better.
- I have time to complete self-evaluation tools for each stage.   ☐ Yes.   ☐ No.
- How can I improve my time management in the next project?

_____

_____

_____

Acknowledgements

The authors and publishers acknowledge the following sources of copyright material and are grateful for the permissions granted. While every effort has been made, it has not always been possible to identify the sources of all the material used, or to trace all copyright holders. If any omissions are brought to our notice, we will be happy to include the appropriate acknowledgements on reprinting and in the next update to the digital edition, as applicable.

Key: Int = Introduction.

Photography

The following photographs are sourced from Getty Images.
Int: Hero Images; kali9/iStock/Getty Images Plus; Snapshots from *Own It Student's Book 4* pp. 22–25, 58, 71; Hill Street Studios/DigitalVision; code6d/E+; ilyast/DigitalVision Vectors; Snapshots from *Own It Student's Book 4* p. 30; SDI Productions/iStock/Getty Images Plus; RobinOlimb/DigitalVision Vectors; Visual Generation/iStock/Getty Images Plus; Wavebreakmedia/iStock/Getty Images Plus; Olivier Verriest/iStock/Getty Images Plus; artursfoto/iStock/Getty Images Plus; vgajic/E+.

Typesetting: TXT Servicios editoriales

Cover design and illustration: Collaborate Agency.

Editing: Andrew Reid